Part of Richard Blome's *New and exact mapp of ye isle of Jamaica* (London 1671)

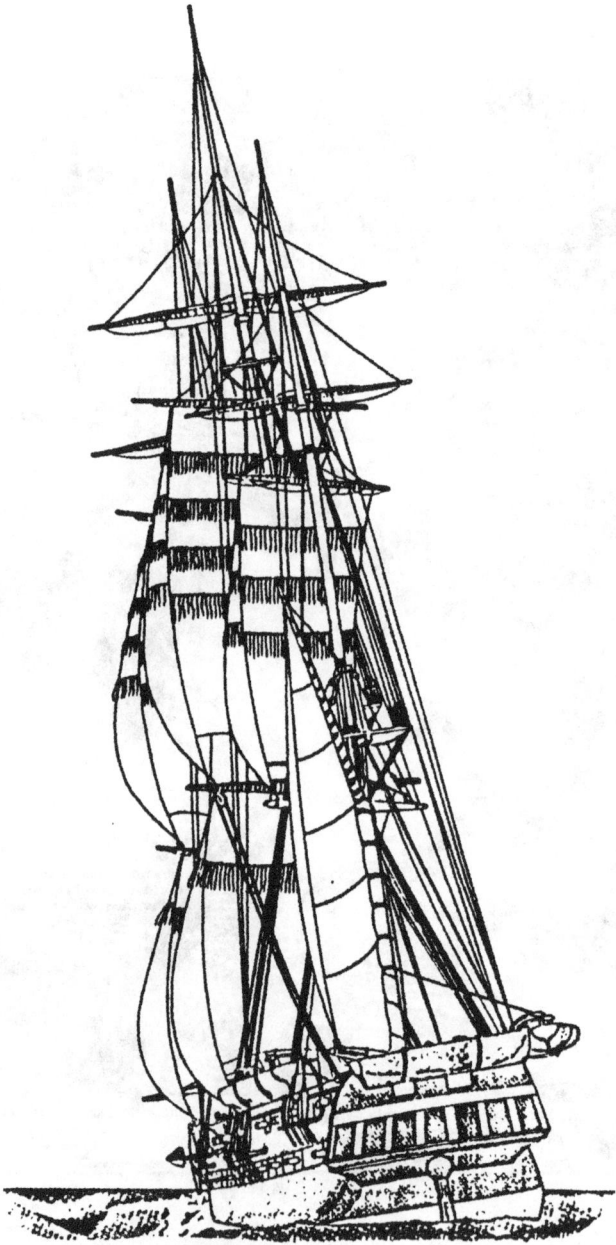

SCOTS
IN THE
WEST INDIES
1707–1857

Volume II

by
David Dobson

CLEARFIELD

Printed for
Clearfield Company, Inc., by
Genealogical Publishing Co., Inc.
Baltimore, Maryland
2006

International Standard Book Number: 0-8063-5312-0

Made in the United States of America

INTRODUCTION

Scotland has had direct social and economic links with the West Indies for nearly 400 years, from the time Spanish power began to wane there in the early seventeenth century. The first vessel known to have sailed from Scotland to the West Indies was named the *Janet of Leith* and left Edinburgh's port of Leith in 1611. Settlement started in 1626 when James Hay, the Scottish Earl of Carlisle, was appointed by King Charles I, Proprietor of Barbados, which in turn led a number of Scots making their way to that island. From Barbados, the English spread their settlements to nearby islands and by the 1650s had taken Jamaica from the Spaniards.

The demand for settlers and servants was met in part by Scottish indentured servants leaving from English ports. Transportees such as Cromwellian prisoners of war, Covenanters and criminals were supplemented by a small flow of emigrants from Glasgow and Edinburgh. Some of the survivors of the ambitious Darien Scheme, whereby Scotland hoped to set up an independent trading post in Panama, arrived in Jamaica and the smaller islands; and Scots could also be found in the Dutch Caribbean islands.

After the union of Scotland and England in 1707, all restrictions on trade between Scotland and the English colonies were lifted. This led to a significant expansion of Scotland's trade with the islands which the English had previously vigorously blocked, and settlement by Scots also increased. In 1763 the French ceded most of their Caribbean islands to the British Crown; and the British expanded into Grenada, Tobago, St.Vincent and Dominica. The West Indian population also increased following the American War of Independence, when many Loyalists, including Scots, took refuge on the islands. Scots also settled in the Danish West Indies.

Although settlement was often more temporary in the islands than in the mainland American colonies, for many. the West Indies offered an opportunity to make or replenish the fortunes of their families. To a larger extent than elsewhere, the colonies of the West Indies attracted Scots with skills or money to invest; and when financial returns were sufficient, they very often returned home to Scotland.

Planters grew sugar cane, cotton and tobacco and produced rum. Mahogany, and other timber, was shipped back to Britain for processing and export to the European markets. Trading links were also expanding with the American mainland, involving the ports of Boston, New York, Philadelphia, Charleston and Savannah. In due course, families moved between these various locations, and links were established.

Glasgow on the Clyde was the main Scottish city to benefit from trade with the West Indies, but others participated. The full impact of Scottish settlement in the economic development of the Caribbean has yet to be fully researched, but the following books provide useful insights – Alan L Karras's *Sojourners in the Sun: Scottish Migrants in Jamaica and the Chesapeake, 1740-1800,* [Cornell, 1992]; Douglas Hamilton's *Scotland, the Caribbean and the Atlantic World, 1750-1820,* [Manchester, 2005]; while an overview may be found in my *Scottish Emigration to Colonial America, 1607-1785,* [Athens, Georgia, 2004].

For those wishing to identify individual Scots who were temporarily or permanently in the West Indies, many can be found in Volume I of *Scots in the West Indies, 1707-1857* or in my earlier works such as *Scottish Settlers in North America, 1625-1825* series; *The Original Scots Colonists: Caribbean Supplement, 1611-1707;* and *Barbados and Scotland, Links 1627-1877;* all published by the Genealogical Publishing Company and Clearfield Publishing in Baltimore.

David Dobson
St Andrews, Scotland

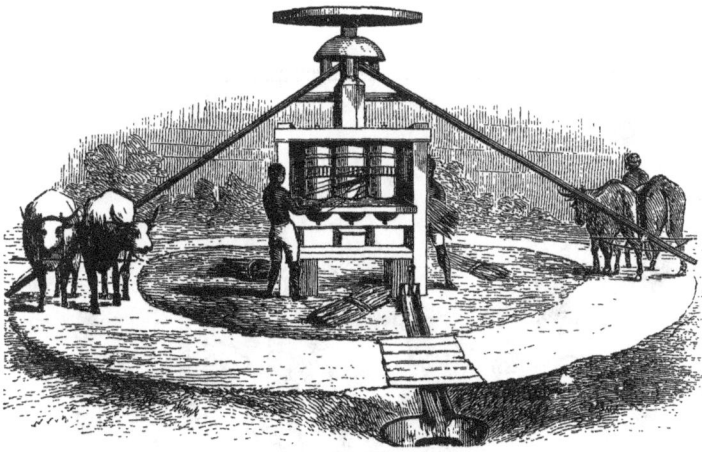

JAMAICA
1774

N

A = Hawthorn Hall
and Moffat's Penn
B = Lucinea Penn

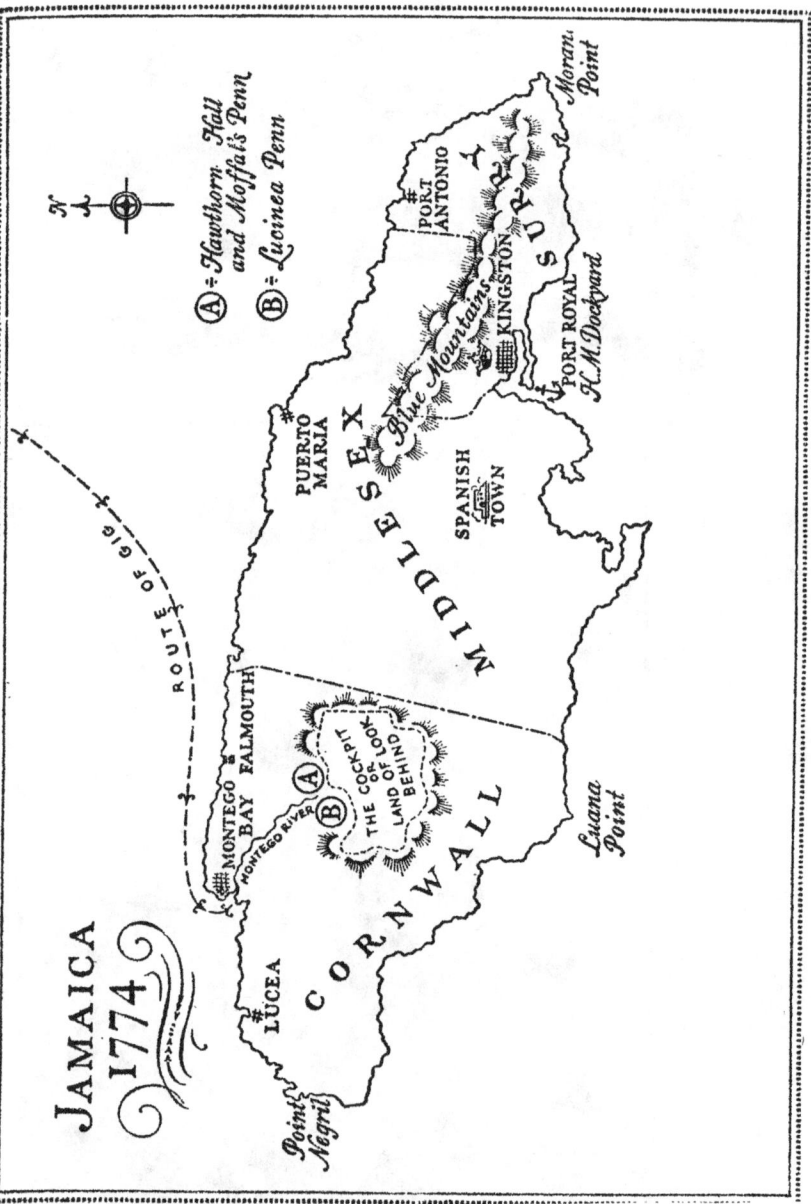

ROUTE OF 1816

Point
Negril

LUCEA

Montego
BAY

FALMOUTH

MONTEGO RIVER

A
B

THE COCKPIT
OR
LAND OF LOOK
BEHIND

CORNWALL

PUERTO
MARIA

MIDDLESEX

Blue Mountains

SPANISH
TOWN

Luana
Point

SURREY

PORT
ANTONIO

KINGSTON

PORT ROYAL
H.M.Dockyard

Morant
Point

REFERENCES

ABR = Ayr Burgess Roll
ACA = Aberdeen City Archives
AJ = Aberdeen Journal, series
AO = Annandale Observer, series
AUL = Aberdeen University Library
AUPC= Annals of the United Presbyterian Church,
        [Edinburgh, 1873]
BS = Bermuda Settlers of the 17th Century, J E Mercer,
        [Baltimore, 1982]
CM = Caledonian Mercury, series
DA = Dundee Archives
EAR = Edinburgh Academy Register
ECA = Edinburgh City Archives
EMG = Edinburgh Medical Graduates, [Edinburgh, 1867]
F = Fasti Ecclesiae Scoticanae, J. Scott,
        [Edinburgh, 1915]
FH Fife Herald, series
GA = Glasgow Archives
GC = Glasgow Courier, series
GkAd= Greenock Advertiser, series
GM = Glasgow Mercury, series
GUL = Glasgow University Library
MC = Montrose Chronicle, series
NAC = National Archives of Cuba, Havanna
NAS = National Archives of Scotland, Edinburgh
NLS = National Library of Scotland, Edinburgh
NRH = New Register House, Edinburgh
Nljam= National Library of Jamaica
PC = Perth Courier, series
PRO = Public Record Office, London
RGG = Roll of Graduates of University of Glasgow
S = Scotsman, series
SP = Scotland and the Protectorate, 1654-1659,
        C. W. Firth, [Edinburgh, 1899]
ST = Scots Times, series
W = Witness, series

SCOTS IN THE WEST INDIES 1707-1857 Volume II

ABERCROMBIE, JOHN, at Montego Bay, Jamaica, 6
   November 1798. [NAS.SC20.33.13]
ABERCROMBIE, WILLIAM, to Jamaica, 1789.
   [NAS.GD171.362]
ABERNETHY, JAMES, a ships carpenter in Jamaica,
   husband of Elizabeth Power, 1778.
   [NAS.CS16.1.173/126]
ADAIR, JOHN, in Grenada, 1777. [NLS#8793]
ADAM, JOHN, from Glasgow, appointed a magistrate in the
   West Indies, 1835. [NAS.GD171.1219]
ADAMSON, ALEXANDER, in Jamaica, 1780.
   [NAS.CS16.1.179]
AFFLECK, DUNCAN, staff surgeon, died in St Vincent on 7
   March 1853. [EEC#22415]
AIKEN, JOHN, a wright in Carncarron Estate, Jamaica, 1799,
   son of John Aitken at Bridge of Johnstone.
   [NAS.CS18.712.13]
AIRD, JOHN, graduated MA, MD, from Glasgow University in
   1772, a practioner of medicine in Antigua. [RGG#7]
AIRD, JOHN MCKENZIE, MCP, married Annette, widow of
   John Cameron, in Tempe House, Grenada, on 11 June
   1863. [S#2521]
AITCHISON, JOHN, from Airdrie, Lanarkshire, died in
   Grenada on 31 May 1780. [Glasgow Mercury#III.286]
AITKEN, PETER, mariner in St Ann's, Middlesex, Jamaica,
   husband of Ann Elizabeth, 1787. [NAS.B56.16.132]

AITKEN, PETER, born in 1834, son of Robert and Anthea Aitken, an engineer, applied to settle in Havana, Cuba, on 15 November 1857. [NAC.Cartas de Domocilio]

ALEXANDER, CHARLES, born in 1822, a merchant from Edinburgh, died in St John, Antigua, 11 December 1860 [S#1748]

ALEXANDER, ELIZABETH, in Aberdeen, relict of Patrick Alexander sometime in Jamaica, testament 2 August 1821 Commissariat of Aberdeen. [NAS.CC...W1050]

ALEXANDER, HUGH, born 1779, eldest son of John Alexander a merchant in Glasgow, died at Edenhill, St Mary's, Jamaica, on 20 September 1802. [GkAd#100]

ALEXANDER, ISOBEL, in Grenada, testament 1869 Edinburgh.[NAS.SC70.1.145/561]

ALEXANDER, JOHN, born in Banffshire during 1800, died on Morne Fendue Estate, Grenada, on 27 March 1840. [AJ#4823]

ALEXANDER, THEODORE, a merchant in Grenada, purchased Westfield, Scotland, on 3 July 1772. [NAS.RGS.112.131][NAS.RS27.200.286]

ALEXANDER, WILLIAM, a merchant in Antigua, 1792. [NAS.RS.Renfrew#3234]

ALEXANDER, WILLIAM, sometime in St Lucia, then on the River Doree, father of Christina and Robertina, 1825. [NAS.RS54.2734/4210]

ALEXANDER, WILLIAM, merchant in St Lucia, owner of the Experiment of Glasgow, 1794. [NAS.CE60.11.4/86]

ALEXANDER & MITCHELL, merchants in Antigua, 1778. [NAS.CS16.1.174]

ALLAN, ALEXANDER, at Montego Bay, Jamaica, died in September 1791, brother of William Allan a shipmaster in Greenock. [NAS.CS26/906.18]

ALLAN, JOHN, a schoolteacher in Kirkcaldy then in Nevis, 1783. [NAS.CS17.1.2/233]

ALLAN, WILLIAM, in Antigua, 1753. [NAS.CS96/645]

ALLAN, WILLIAM, only son of John Allan a merchant in Tortula, matriculated at Glasgow University in 1801. [MAGU#197]

ALLARDICE, JOHN, born 1798, died 19 February 1823. [Palisades gravestone, Port Royal, Jamaica]

ALLARDYCE, ALEXANDER, in Jamaica, then in Dunottar, Kincardineshire, 20 December 1782.

[NAS.RGS.121.149]

ALLARDYCE, JAMES, in Jamaica, 1806. [NAS.GD171.844]

ALLASON, JOHN, a merchant in St Kitts, son of Thomas
Allason a merchant in Glasgow, 1782, 1786.
[NAS.CS17.1.1/243; 5/278]

ALSTON, JAMES, in Spanish Town, Jamaica, 1800.
[NAS.GD1.394.54]

ALVES, THOMAS, in Spanish Town, Jamaica, 1786; at
Montego Bay, Jamaica, 1792.
[NAS.GD23.6.441; RS38.PR15/518]

AMORY, JOSEPH, eldest son of Joseph Amory a merchant in
St Kitts, matriculated at Glasgow University in 1793.
[MAGU#172]

ANDERSON, ALEXANDER, born 1748, educated at
Edinburgh University, to New York in 1774, to Surinam
during the American Revolution but taken prisoner by a
privateer and landed on Martinique, settled in St Lucia,
later a botanist in St Vincent, died in 1811.

ANDERSON, ALEXANDER, in Hanover parish, Jamaica,
later in Udall, 1814. [NAS.RS.Cromarty#223]

ANDERSON, DUNCAN, born 1757 in Stenton, East Lothian,
died in 1796. [St James gravestone, Montego Bay,
Jamaica]

ANDERSON, JAMES, educated at Marischal College,
Aberdeen, around 1737, settled in Jamaica, graduated
MD on 22 September 1755 and M.Corp.S. in 1761 from
Marischal College, Aberdeen. [AUL]

ANDERSON, Dr JAMES, in St Kitts then in Midmiln of
Cruden, 20 December 1800. [RGS#132/34/35]

ANDERSON, JOHN, in St Kitts, 1802. [NAS.RS8.PR34.392]

ANDERSON, JOHN, surgeon in Jamaica, dead by 1783.
[NAS.CS17.1.2/245]

ANDERSON, ROBERT BRUNTON, MD, born 1820, died in
Jamaica on 5 December 1842. [Dean gravestone,
Edinburgh]

ANDERSON, THOMAS, West Indies, graduated MD from
Edinburgh University in 1815. [EMG#49]

ANDERSON, WILLIAM, from St Croix, died in Lenzie on 11
October 1878. [EC#29343]

ANDERSON, Dr....., 'a Scots gentleman who went abroad 25
years ago', died in St Kitts 1736. [EEC#1987]

ANDERSON, ..., from Inverness, a magistrate in Kingston,
St Vincent, in 1838. [AJ#4719]

ANDERSON, ..., son of Izett W. Anderson MD, was born in Kingston, Jamaica, on 10 September 1873. [EC#27790]

ANGUS, WILLIAM, of Montego Bay, Jamaica, son of Alexander Angus a bookseller in Aberdeen, died at sea off Port Antonio in 1807. [DPCA#267]

ARCHER, JAMES, second son of George Archer a physician in Jamaica, matriculated at Glasgow University in 1812. [MAGU#266]

ARCHIBALD, CHARLES, second son of S. G. Archibald, 22 Windsor St., Edinburgh, died on Plaisance Estate, Trinidad, 12 May 1869. [S#8073]

ARMSTRONG, GEORGE, eldest son of Archibald Armstrong a gentleman in Grenada, matriculated at Glasgow University in 1808. [MAGU#238]

ARMSTRONG, GEORGE, second son of Archibald Armstrong a merchant in St George's, Grenada, matriculated at Glasgow University in 1809. [MAGU#238]

ARMSTRONG, JEAN, in Antigua, 1753. [NAS.CS96/645]

ARMSTRONG, WILLIAM, a gentleman in St Kitts, surgeon to the Naval Hospital in St Kitts, graduated MD in Aberdeen on 18 October 1798. [AUL]

ARMSTRONG, WILLIAM, in St Croix, 1801. [NLS.MS5602/3]

ARTHUR, WILLIAM, in Antigua 1753. [NAS.CS96/644]

AUCHTERLONY, ALEXANDER, settled in Dominica 1765. [NAS.GD126, box 4]

AUCHTERLONY, JOHN, a silk dyer in Kingston, Jamaica, 10 January 1827. [NAS.RS.Edinburgh.29/243]

AUGHTERSON, JAMES, Special Chief Justice, died in Castries, St Lucia, on 21 November 1838. [SG#8/738]

AULD, ROBERT, in Tobago, testament 1864 Edinburgh. [NAS.SC70.1.10/809]

BAILLIE, ALEXANDER, of Dochfour, in Grenada, 1800. [NAS.GD23.6.477]

BAILLIE, DAVID, a planter at Auchensheoch Estate, Tobago, 1836. [NA.T71/1572]

BAILLIE, EVAN, in St Vincent, granted lands of Kynmylies on 23 February 1776. [NAS.RGS.116.101]

BAILLIE, GRANT, born 1812, second son of John Baillie in Roehampton, Jamaica, died on Carawina Estate, Westmoreland, Jamaica, on 18 March 1854. [EEC#22572]

BAILLIE, JAMES, a merchant in Jamaica, 1740, son of
Robert Baillie a merchant in Edinburgh.
[NAS.GD1.1155.64]

BAILLIE, ROBERT, a merchant in Jamaica, late a planter in
Georgia, 1750, son of George Baillie of Hardington.
[NAS.GD1.1155.65]

BAIRD, ANTONY, third son of Daniel Baird a merchant in St
Kitts, matriculated at Glasgow University in 1808.
[MAGU#235]

BAIRD, CHARLES, in Antigua, 1775. [AUL.ms3175/668, 3]

BAIRD, DANIEL, second son of Daniel Baird a merchant in St
Kitts, matriculated at Glasgow University in 1808.
[MAGU#235]

BAIRD, GEORGE, a merchant in Kingston, Jamaica, 1760,
1778. [AUL.ms3175,668, 3; bundle 4]

BAIRD, JOHN, at Plantation Montreuil, parish of St Patrick,
Grenada, 1792. [NAS.GD237.12.52]

BAIRD, WILLIAM, at Plantation Montreuil, parish of St
Patrick, Grenada, 1792. [NAS.GD237.12.52]

BALDERSTON, GEORGE, a surgeon in Edinburgh later in St
Kitts, deceased by 1767, husband of Euphan Douglas.
[NAS.RS27.177.244]

BALDIE, JOHN, in Jamaica, deceased, 1798.
[NAS.SC20.33.13]

BALFOUR, CHARLES, late in Jamaica, died in Cardrona on
29 October 1786. [GM#IX.462.355]

BALFOUR, JOHN, a merchant in Glasgow, and his wife Janet
Corbett, late in Jamaica, granted lands of Kenmuir on 2
June 1813. [NAS.RGS.148.55]; May 1814,
[NAS.CS17.1.34/401]

BALFOUR, WILLIAM, at Montego Bay, Jamaica, 1788, 1792.
[NAS.RS.Caithness#101/224]

BALFOUR, WILLIAM, Martha Brae, Jamaica, died on 9
January 1804. [CM#121875]

BALLANTINE, JAMES, a merchant from Southbridge,
Edinburgh, then in St Vincent, 1802. [NAS.AC7.75]

BALLANTYNE, PATRICK, merchant in Kingston, Jamaica,
co-owner of the Mercury of Glasgow 1795.
[NAS.CE60.11.4/21]

BANNATYNE, JAMES, late a writer in Edinburgh, then in
Jamaica, 1783. [NAS.CS17.1.2/256]

BARBOUR, JOHN, a merchant from Glasgow, in St Vincent,
1834. [NAS.SC58.59.14.89]

BARCLAY, ANDREW, born 1791, a Presbyterian resident of St Croix, Danish West Indies, 1841. [1841 Census]

BARCLAY, DUNCAN, died in Jamaica 1735. [NAS.GD170.3089]

BARCLAY, GEORGE, from Cairnes, Peterhead, Aberdeenshire, settled in Jamaica before 1727. [AUL.MS1160.5.2/11]

BARCLAY, GEORGE, a burgess and guildsbrother of Aberdeen, a merchant in Jamaica, 1741. [NAS.GD67.93]

BARCLAY, HENRY, late of Dunbar, died at the Hermitage, Jamaica, on 3 May 1860. [DC#23505]

BARCLAY, JAMES, emigrated in 1727, a book-keeper in Kingston, Jamaica, 1729, by 1762 was the Auditor Receiver General there. [AUL.MS1160/5,2,3] [NAS.GD67.34, 35, 37]

BARCLAY, JAMES, planter of 30 acres, St Andrew's parish, Jamaica, 1754. [NA.CO137/28]

BARCLAY, ROBINA, or TURNBULL, in Jamaica, 21 August 1810. [NAS.RS.Edinburgh.2/95]

BARKER, JOHN, a merchant in Kingston, Jamaica, 1778. [NAS.CS16.1.173/159]

BARR, JOHN RITCHIE, in Jamaica, 1813. [NAS.RS54.PR146/75]

BARR, ROBERT MACAULAY, born 1811, a planter, died in Grenada on 12 December 1867. [S#7635]

BATHGATE, WILLIAM, a writer in Edinburgh who indented with John McLeod a merchant in Edinburgh, to serve in Jamaica for four years, 3 September 1736. [NAS.RH19/17/316]

BAYNE, Reverend JAMES, of Mount Zion Church, Jamaica, married Agnes Barr Grant, youngest daughter of Alexander Grant of Spot Valley Estate, at Mount Zion on 31 January 1878. [EC#29151]

BEDDIE, BENJAMIN, manager on Clare Valley Estate, St Vincent, died 28 September 1810. [Wigtown gravestone]

BEGG, JOHN, Jamaica, graduated MD from Edinburgh University in 1793. [EMG#24]

BELL, ALEXANDER, in Jamaica, was admitted as a burgess and guilds-brother of Ayr on 27 July 1776. [ABR]

BELL, Dr ALLAN, second son of Hugh Bell, Half Merkland, Dalrymple, Ayrshire, died in Jamaica on 18 June 1845. [SG#14/1424]

BENNET, GEORGE WILLIAM, married Elizabeth Burns, third daughter of Patrick Burns of Villa Estate, in Antigua on 5 February 1861. [S#1841]

BENNET, JAMES, son of John Bennet {1764-1827}, a farmer in Finnartbeg, and Agnes Anderson {1770-1830}, died in the West Indies during 1820. [Kilmun, gravestone, Argyll]

BENNET, MAXWELL, a writer in Edinburgh then Jamaica, 1780. [NAS.CS16.1.179]

BERRIE, JAMES, third son of Robert Berrie a judge in the West Indies, matriculated at Glasgow University in 1806. [MAGU#223]

BERRIE, ROBERT, second son of Robert Berrie a judge in the West Indies, matriculated at Glasgow University in 1806. [MAGU#223]

BERTRAM, JOHN, in Tobago, 1777, brother of William Bertram of Nisbet. [NAS.GD5.460]

BISSET, JAMES, born in 1843, son of William Bisset in Upperkirkgate, Aberdeen, died in Grenada on 10 May 1865. [AJ:21.6.1865]

BLACK, Captain ARCHIBALD, born in Greenock, died in St Domingo on 21 July 1825. [Blackwood's Magazine#XVIII.779]

BLACK, JAMES, factor in Nassau, New Providence, 1799. [NAS.CS96.1293]

BLACK, JAMES MCNAIR, third son of John Black a merchant in Manchester late in Glasgow, died in Havanna on 14 August 1849. [SG#18/1848]

BLACK, JOHN, a merchant in Trinidad, eldest son of the late George Black and heir to Dr Joseph Black who died 1799. [NAS.CS18.715.16]

BLACK, JOHN, in Jamaica, 1818. [NAS.RS.Argyll#2991]

BLACK, JOHN, from Dunfermline, died in Antigua 22 August 1840. [W#83]

BLACK, ROBERT, a surgeon in Jamaica, son of James Black a leather cutter and merchant in Glasgow, 1799. [NAS.CS26.908.13]

BLACKADDER, WILLIAM, in Antigua 1758. [DA.Ogilvie pp/25]

BLACKBURN, JOHN, a planter in St Thomas in the Vale, Jamaica, 1803, [NAS.RH15.76.23]; from Levenside late in Jamaica, granted lands of Killearn on 5 July 1813. [NAS.RGS.148.17]

BLAIR, DAVID, naval officer at St Lucia, 1798.
[NAS.GD1/884/2]

BLAIR, DUNCAN, eldest son of John Blair a farmer in
Drymen, Stirlingshire, matriculated at Glasgow
University in 1810, possibly the Duncan Blair from
Gartmore, Stirlingshire, who died on Carriacou in 1855
aged 62. [MAGU#249]

BLAIR, JOHN, planter of 214 acres, St Andrew's parish,
Jamaica, 1754. [NA.CO137/28]

BLANE, JOHN, a merchant in Antigua 1751.
[NAS.RD2.211.1.380]; from Ayrshire, died in Antigua
1755. [GJ#756]

BLAW, JAMES, a surgeon in Jamaica, probably from
Kirkwall, 1780. [NAS.CS16.1.177]

BLYTH, JOHN, born 1774, son of John Blyth a merchant in
Old Meldrum, Aberdeenshire, died in Falmouth,
Jamaica, in 1809. [PC#61]

BOGLE, ANDREW, merchant in Jamaica, co-owner of the
Magnet of Glasgow, 1800. [NAS.CE60.11.6/18]; in
Kingston, Jamaica, 1809, [NAS.NRAS#0063]; late in
Jamaica, granted land in Provan on 2 June 1817.
[NAS.RGS.155.74]

BOGLE, ROBERT, jr, in Grenada, 1776. [NLS.Acc8793/12]

BONTEIN, THOMAS, in Jamaica, 1749. [NAS.RD2.168.145]

BORTHWICK, GEORGE, a smith later of Jamaica, now in
Fountainbridge, Edinburgh, 1799. [NAS.CS22.776.8]

BOTHWELL, WILLIAM, surgeon on board HMS Tweed, died
in the West Indies on 24 July 1834. [AJ#4530]

BOWES, ELLEN M., wife of Colonel J. A. Mein of the 74th
Regiment, died in Trinidad on 20 May 1840.
[AJ#4829][W#55]

BOWHILL, ..., son of James Bowhill, was born on 11 March
1861 at Riseland Estate, Tobago. [S#1809]

BOWIE, JAMES, in Antigua, 1753. [NAS.CS96/645]

BOWIE, WILLIAM, late in Antigua, son of John Bowie a
merchant in Ayr, was admitted as a burgess and guilds-
brother of Ayr on 24 September 1790. [ABR]

BOYD, HUGH, in Antigua 1759. [DA.Ogilvie pp/29]

BOYD, MARY, Jamaica, married Robert Kalley a merchant in
Glasgow, on 3 August 1795. [GM#65/702]

BOYLE, JAMES LAWRENCE, son of John Boyle, a merchant
in St Croix, 1779, [NAS.CS16.1.175]; 1800.
[NAS.CS17.1.19/350]

BRANCH, TOM MACINTOSH, born in 1861, son of John Ames Branch, died on Camp Estate, St Kitts, on 5 January 1876. [EC#288498]

BRANDS, JAMES, eldest son of James Brands of Old Ferryhill (1703-1780) and Ann Stewart (1710-1793), died at Montego Bay, Jamaica, 1794. [St Nicholas gravestone, Aberdeen]

BRANDS, ROBERT, MD, in Jamaica, 1786. [NAS.RS38.PR30/170]; youngest son of James Brands of Ferry Hill, Aberdeen, and Anne Stewart, died in Hanover, Jamaica, on 13 December 1788. [GM#XII.582.69]; Dr Robert Brands, Caledonia estate, Jamaica, youngest son of James Brands of Old Ferryhill (1703-1780) and Ann Stewart (1710-1793), died in 1788. [St Nicholas gravestone, Aberdeen]

BRASH, FRANCIS BANKS, born 1843, son of Alexander Brash and his wife Agnes Denham, a sugar plantation manager in Trinidad, married Jane Graham McNee, born 1841 daughter of Duncan McNee and his wife Elizabeth Marshall, in Glasgow on 22 January 1867, died on Lothians Estate, Trinidad, on 21 March 1892. [Glasgow, Anderston, 1861/28] [Trinidad, Savannah Grande#1892/486]

BRASS, ..., son of Robert S. Brass, was born on 4 March 1869 at 26 High Holborn Street, Kingston, Jamaica. [S#8013]

BRAYNAN, JAMES, from Scotland, was admitted as a burgher of St Eustatia, DWI, on 8 December 1780. [NA.CO318.8.84v]

BREARCLIFFE, DONALD, born in 1788, son of Matthew Brearcliffe {1748-1824} and Catherine ..... {1750-1829}, died in Jamaica on 24 October 1867. [Wigtown gravestone]

BREMNER, WILLIAM, Jamaica, graduated MD from Edinburgh University in 1818. [EMG#55]

BRITTARGH, WILLIAM, a Jacobite rebel, transported from London to Antigua on the <u>Prince George</u>, master James Nairn, on 14 January 1748, landed 16 March 1748. [NA.T53/44]

BRODIE, Reverend GEORGE, born in 1815, a missionary of the United Presbyterian Church, died in Port of Spain, Trinidad, on 7 October 1875. [EC#28419]

BROWN, CHARLES, Jamaica, graduated MD from Edinburgh University in 1797. [EMG#28]

BROWN, DUNCAN, merchant in Kingston, St George's, St Vincent, 1822. [NAS.AC7.100.1019]

BROWN, JAMES, son of Alexander Brown, Knockollochy, Chapel of Garioch, Aberdeenshire, died at Montego Bay, Jamaica, on 12 August 1848. [AJ:4.10.1848]

BROWN, JOHN, from Elgin, Morayshire, a surveyor in Tobago, 1780. [NLS.MS2385/2, 7]

BROWN, JOHN, a mariner in Kingston, St George's, St Vincent, then a shipmaster in Greenock, 1822. [NAS.AC7.100.1019]

BROWN, JONATHAN, born 1783, died in Jamaica on 13 November 1843. [Wigtown gravestone]

BROWN, JOSIAS, from Glasgow, a Wesleyan missionary in St Vincent, married Martha Amelia, youngest daughter of Captain J. Keens from Bristol, in Tobago on 4 January 1842. [GSP#707]

BROWN, PATRICK, born in 1768, died in Nassau, New Providence, on 15 June 1845. [SG#14/128]

BROWN, WILLIAM, from Glasgow, a merchant in St Kitts, then a planter at Lower Quarter Plantation, St David's parish, Tobago, 1764. [GA:B10.15.7493]

BROWN, WILLIAM, a planter in Jamaica, son of James Brown a shipmaster in Dundee, 1781. [DCA: H4511]

BRUCE, ALEXANDER, in Jamaica, dead by 1768. [NAS.GD237.21.51/11]

BRUCE, ALEXANDER, born 1818, son of William Bruce in Langholm, died in St Vincent 1851. [Dundonald gravestone]

BRUCE, ALEXANDER, born 1836, son of James Bruce (1792-1864) and Janet McDonald (1805-1876), died in Jamaica in September 1864. [Tomnacross gravestone, Inverness-shire]

BRUCE, JAMES, a merchant in Dominica, son of Captain James Bruce of the 26th Regiment, 18 August 1791. [NAS.SC20.36.15]

BRUCE, JOHN, a merchant in Grenada, then in Edinburgh, 1821. [NAS.CS17.1.40/271]

BRUCE, Sir MICHAEL, a planter on Shewan Estate, Tobago, 1836. [NA.T71/1572]

BRUCE, ROBERT GEORGE, an engineer in Dominica, 1776. [NAS.GD20.1.384]

BRUCE, THOMAS, in St Vincent, son of David Bruce of Kinnaird, died in Edinburgh on 24 January 1789. [GM#XII.579.38]

BRUCE, Dr WILLIAM, an army physician, died in the West Indies 1780. [Glasgow Mercury#III.149]

BRYCE, JOHN, Montego Bay, Jamaica, married Jane, eldest daughter of James Mitchell an engineer, at York Place, Glasgow, on 31 October 1839. [SG#8/817]

BRYDEN, JAMES, born in 1811, son of David Bryden a millwright in Douglas, Lanarkshire, died in Trinidad on 21 December 1838. [SG#8/745]

BRYDIE, WILLIAM, a merchant in Jamaica, 1796. [NAS.CS17.1.15/216]

BUCHAN, WILLIAM, from Stirling, later in St Thomas, Jamaica, 1810. [NAS.SC67.49.1/185]

BUCHANAN, ALEXANDER, sometime in Tobago late in Campbeltown, Argyll, edict of executry, 1811. [NAS.CC2.8.115, 13]

BUCHANAN, ARCHIBALD SHANNAN, of Drumhead, Dunbartonshire, died in Antigua on 18 September 1791. [Glasgow Courier#35]

BUCHANAN, COLIN, in Barbados, father of Colin born 1818 and Arthur born 1820, both educated at Edinburgh Academy from 1828 to 1829. [EAR]

BUCHANAN, JAMES, a planter in Jamaica, then in America, 1801. [NAS.CS17.1.20/14]

BUCHANAN, WALTER, eldest son of William Buchanan, late of the 1st Royal Veteran Battalion, died in Spanish Town, Jamaica, on 22 October 1838. [SG#8/735]

BUNTEIN, THOMAS, sometime in Port Royal, Jamaica, son of Robert Bontein of Mildowan, 1754. [NAS.CS16.1.92/266]

BURNET, JOHN, in Kingston, Jamaica, 30 November 1716. [BM.Sloane#4044/250]

BURNET, ..., daughter of George Burnet in Jamaica, buried in St Nicholas churchyard, Aberdeen, 25 November 1755. [ACA]

BURNETT, THEODOSIUS, in Dominica, brother of John Burnett a merchant in Aberdeen, 1783. [NAS.GD23.3.51]

BURNETT, WILLIAM, in Antigua 1758. [DA.Ogilvie pp/26]

BURNETT, ..., planter of 502 acres, St Andrew's parish, Jamaica, 1754. [NA.CO137/28]

BURNS, ROBERT, son of Patrick Burns in St Andrews, Fife, died in Antigua on 8 July 1867. [S#7491]

BURNSIDE, THOMAS, planter of 480 acres, St Andrew's parish, Jamaica, 1754. [NA.CO.137/28]

BURNTFIELD, DAVID, born 1808, son of George Burntfield and Lillie Stewart, died in Dominica 4 June 1838. [Greyfriars gravestone, Perth]

BURT, ..., son of Archibald P. Burt, QC, was born in St Kitts on 18 March 1867. [S#7396]

BYGRAVE, ANN, wife of Reverend J.M.Frew, Rector of St Thomas in the East, Jamaica, died 29 March 1842. [GSP#718]

CAIRD, HENRY WILLIAM, MA, born in 1833, second master of Queen's Royal College, Port of Spain, Trinidad, died there on 16 March 1878. [EC#29193]

CAIRNS, WALTER HENDERSON, son of Thomas Cairns, 53 Home Street, Edinburgh, died in St Thomas, West Indies, on 13 January 1867. [S#7336]

CALDER, GEORGE, only son of George Calder a merchant in Jamaica, matriculated at Glasgow University in 1806. [MAGU#222]

CALLUM, ALEXANDER, sometime a clerk to Campbell, Ruthven and Lindsay merchants in Greenock, then a merchant in Jamaica, 1804. [NAS.AC7/77]

CAMERON, ALEXANDER, in Jamaica, natural son of John Cameron, {no date}. [NAS.PS3.13/103]

CAMERON, ARCHIBALD, from Lochaber, emigrated from Scotland on 10 October 1764, arrived in Jamaica on 21 December 1764. [AUL.BDpp/H1766/01]

CAMERON, HUGH, servant to Edward Garvine a merchant in St Kitts, was admitted as a burgess and guildsbrother of Ayr on 3 October 1737. [ABR]

CAMPBELL, ALEXANDER, in Port Royal, Jamaica, around 1736. [NAS.GD170.735]

CAMPBELL, ALEXANDER, a merchant in Tobago, 1776. [NA.T1.527.271-272]

CAMPBELL, ALEXANDER, in Islay then in Jamaica, 1780. [NAS.CS16.1.179]

CAMPBELL, ALEXANDER, at Green River, Jamaica, 1780. [NAS.CS16.1.179]

CAMPBELL, Dr ALEXANDER, of Lancet Hall, late of St Ann's parish, Jamaica, died in Edinburgh on 15 February 1792. [GCr#75][EEC:18.2.1792]

CAMPBELL, ALEXANDER, a surgeon late of Kingston, Jamaica, second son of the late Alexander Campbell, 1782. [NAS.CS17.1.1/20]

CAMPBELL, ALEXANDER, only son of Reverend Colin Campbell rector of St Andrews, Jamaica, matriculated at Glasgow University in 1792. [MAGU#168]

CAMPBELL, ALEXANDER, of Maran, Grenada, 1803. [NAS.GD112/61/2]

CAMPBELL, ALEXANDER BOWERBANK, MD, son of Reverend John Campbell in Jamaica, died at Stoney Hill, Jamaica, on 12 September 1879. [EC#29653]

CAMPBELL, ANGUS, son of Campbell of Fornighty, a Captain of the 37th Regiment, died in St Vincnet in 1801. [EEC:30.7.1801]

CAMPBELL, ANN, relict of William McDonald a planter in Jamaica, 1768. [NAS.RS27.179.206, 211]

CAMPBELL, Mrs ANN, wife of James McNeilledge in St Croix, died 24 August 1803. [EEC]

CAMPBELL, ARCHIBALD, a merchant in Kingston, Jamaica, 1788. [NAS.RS.Glasgow#1045/1050]

CAMPBELL, ARCHIBALD, eldest son of Ronald Campbell a merchant in Campbeltown later in Jamaica and his wife Jean, emigrated to the West Indies in 1790. [Argyll Sheriff Court Book #XIX,12.5.1790]

CAMPBELL, ARCHIBALD, of Providence Estate, Macheneill, Jamaica, 31 December 1793, only son of John Campbell, merchant in Greenock later tacksman of Larkfield, Innerkip, Renfrewshire, and his wife Jean Campbell. [NAS/SC58.58.7]

CAMPBELL, ARCHIBALD, of Nassau, died 4 June 1798. [EEC: 9.8.1798]

CAMPBELL, CHARLES, MD, in Kingston, Jamaica, testament 1873 Edinburgh. [NAS.SC70.1.164/729]

CAMPBELL, CHARLES, born in 1853, fourth son of Archibald Campbell a feuar and shipowner in Lochgilphead, Argyll, died in Clarksonville, Alexandria, Jamaica, on 5 November 1878. [EC#29391]

CAMPBELL, COLIN, jr., a merchant in Glasgow now in Jamaica, 1785. [NAS.CS17.1.4/344]

CAMPBELL, COLIN, late merchant in Greenock, then in Holland's estate, St Elizabeth parish, Cornwall County, Jamaica, husband of Henrietta, daughter of Duncan Campbell, who were married in Glasgow in August

1776, Process of Divorce 1790. [Commissariat of Edinburgh]

CAMPBELL, COLIN, deceased, formerly a merchant in Jamaica, brother of Elizabeth Campbell, both children of Archibald Campbell of Barnacraig, 1789. [Argyll Sheriff Court Book #XIX]

CAMPBELL, COLIN, jr., settled in Hanover, Jamaica, 1794. [NAS.GD1.512.15][NAS.GD1.512.26]

CAMPBELL, COLIN, Jamaica, graduated MD from Edinburgh University in 1812. [EMG#45]

CAMPBELL, DANIEL, planter of 98 acres, St Andrew's parish, Jamaica, 1754. [NA.CO137/28]

CAMPBELL, DAVID, in St Thomas in the Vale, Jamaica, 1762. [Argyll Sheriff Court Book, #XVI]

CAMPBELL, Dr DAVID, a physician in Jamaica, brother of John Campbell of Glen Lyon, 1781. [NAS.GD155/287]

CAMPBELL, DONALD, a planter, St Mary's, Jamaica, 1777. [Argyll Sheriff Court Deeds, 9.7.1781]

CAMPBELL, DONALD, in Jamaica, 1780. [NAS.CS16.1.179]

CAMPBELL, DONALD, Secretary to the Governor, Spanish Town, Jamaica, 1784. [NAS.GD461.56]

CAMPBELL, DONALDSON, in Grenada, 1795. [NAS.GD18/3532]

CAMPBELL, DUGALD, a merchant in Kingston, Jamaica, son of Colin Campbell the Customs Controller in Campbeltown, Argyll, edict of executry, 1801. [NAS.CC2.8.105, 9]

CAMPBELL, DUGALD, fourth son of Archibald Campbell of Lerags, died in Jamaica in 1816. [S#15]

CAMPBELL, DUNCAN, partner in the merchant house of McDuffie and Campbell in Jamaica, 1771. [NAS.CS16.1.143/128]

CAMPBELL, DUNCAN, in St Vincent, 1776. [NLS.Acc8793/6]; in St Vincent, 1779, brother of Mary Campbell at Ardnave. [Argyll Sheriff Court Deeds, 21.6.1787]

CAMPBELL, DUNCAN, of Knapdale, died in Jamaica 1795. [EEC:21.12.1795]

CAMPBELL, DUNCAN, Morvern, Hanover parish, Jamaica, died 9 September 1810. [EEC]

CAMPBELL, DUNCAN, of Culchena, died in Campbelton, Jamaica, in 1817. [S#5]

CAMPBELL, Dr D. MCEACHERN, died in Lucca, Jamaica, on 24 June 1814. [EEC]

CAMPBELL, GRACE BUCHANAN, daughter of Colin Campbell in Jamaica, wife of Robert Stevens, a solicitor in Edinburgh, 3 February 1818. [NAS.RGS.157.23.52]

CAMPBELL, HUGH, a merchant burgess of Edinburgh, son of James Campbell a merchant burgess of Edinburgh, settled in Bermuda by July 1679, moved to Norfolk, Virginia, by 1688. [BS]

CAMPBELL, Colonel JAMES, born 1697, died 13 July 1744. [Orange Bay Estate gravestone, Jamaica]

CAMPBELL, JAMES, in Jamaica, admitted as a burgess of Glasgow on 8 March 1717. [Glasgow Burgess Roll]

CAMPBELL, JAMES, a Jacobite rebel, transported from Liverpool to Jamaica on the <u>Elizabeth</u>, master Daniel Cole, on 7 February 1748, landed 21 March 1748. [NA.T53/44]

CAMPBELL, JAMES, of Kames, Cowal, late merchant in Glasgow, sometime in Jamaica, late in Rothesay, testament confirmed on 23 July 1761 with the Commissariat of the Isles. [NAS]

CAMPBELL, JAMES, in Snowhill, near Kingston, Jamaica, 1768. [NAS.GD237.21.51/11]

CAMPBELL, JAMES, late a merchant in Kingston, Jamaica, then in Crieff, 1771. [NAS.CS16.1.143/128]

CAMPBELL, JAMES, in Grenada, 1776. [NLS.Acc.8793/52]

CAMPBELL, JAMES, Dowan Vale, Jamaica, was admitted as a burgess of Banff in 1783. [Banff Burgess Roll]

CAMPBELL, JAMES, late planter in Tobago, then in Rothesay, testament confirmed on 10 June 1784 with the Commissariat of the Isles. [NAS]

CAMPBELL, JAMES, late in Tobago, died 29 March 1801. [EEC]

CAMPBELL, JAMES, of Ormaig, Captain of a troop of native cavalry during the late insurrection in St Vincent and Grenada, died 21 April 1805. [EEC]

CAMPBELL, JAMES, Argyll Estate, Tobago, died 13 October 1805. [EEC]

CAMPBELL, JAMES, late of Grenada, died 3 May 1810. [EEC]

CAMPBELL, JAMES, born 6 August 1829 at Moor Park, Lanarkshire, son of James Murdoch Campbell and

Elizabeth Bogle, died at Mount Pleasant, St Vincent, on 14 May 1845. [Dean gravestone, Edinburgh]

CAMPBELL, JAMES, born in 1834, an engineer, applied to settle in Cienfuegos, Cuba, on 9 December 1857. [NAC.Cartas de Domocilio]

CAMPBELL, Captain JOHN, born 1700, died 29 July 1766. [Orange Bay Estate gravestone, Jamaica]

CAMPBELL, JOHN, a merchant in Tobago, 1776. [NA.T1.527.271-272]

CAMPBELL, JOHN, Lanathall, married Elizabeth Bell from Glasgow, in Jamaica during 1790. [GM.60.1213]

CAMPBELL, JOHN, late in Grenada then in Perth, son of John Campbell a merchant in Perth, testament 7 April 1796 St Andrews; executor of Mrs Ann Campbell, edict of executry 1801. [NAS.CC2.8.105, 3]

CAMPBELL, JOHN, Captain of the Royal Artillery, died near Kingston, Jamaica, on 30 May 1805. [EEC]

CAMPBELL, JOHN, of Orange Bay, born 1732, former Custos Rotulorum of Hanover parish, Cornwall County, Jamaica, died 16 May 1808. [Orange Bay Estate gravestone, Jamaica]

CAMPBELL, JOHN, St Mary's parish, Jamaica, 12 May 1813. [NAS.RD.Argyll#1/112]

CAMPBELL, LACHLAN, son of Campbell of Craignish, died 8 September on the De Caleman on his passage home from Tobago, edict of executry 1785. [NAS.CC2.8.88, 6]

CAMPBELL, LYDIA, a planter on Lower Quarter Estate, Tobago, 1836. [NA.T71/1572]

CAMPBELL, MARION, eldest daughter of Thomas Campbell, 12 George Square, Edinburgh, married James Mayer Grant, Colonial Treasurer, in Calligua, St Vincent, on 20 June 1855. [EEC#22768]

CAMPBELL, MARK, only son of late Dr Alexander Campbell in Dunkeld, Perthshire, died in Grenada on 2 December 1791. [GCr#90][EEC:24.3.1792]

CAMPBELL, Mrs MARY, of Elister, died in Jamaica 1795. [EEC:21.11.1795]

CAMPBELL, MUNGO, late in Grenada, then in Edinburgh, was admitted as a burgess and guilds-brother of Ayr on 2 October 1780. [ABR]

CAMPBELL, NEILL, in Antigua 1753. [NAS.CS96/644]

CAMPBELL, Dr PATRICK [PETER], in Jamaica, 1779, son of Captain Duncan Campbell of Edinburgh City Guard.

[NAS.CS16.1.175]; late in Jamaica, died at Liberton Kirk on 15 December 1785. [GM#IX.468.413][EEC]; later in Liberton, testament confirmed with the Commissariat of Edinburgh on 2 March 1787. [NAS]

CAMPBELL, PRYSE JOHN, died in the West Indies in August 1795. [EEC:7.11.1795]

CAMPBELL, REBECCA, daughter of Colin Campbell in Jamaica, relict of Adam Scott of Roundhill, Jamaica, granted lands of Lumloch on 3 February 1818. [NAS.RGS.157.23.52]

CAMPBELL, ROBERT STEVENSON, fifth son of Reverend John Campbell minister of the Secession Church, Nicholson Street, Lauriston, died in Nevis on 23 September 1839. [SG#8/820]

CAMPBELL, SUSANNA, daughter of Colin Campbell in Jamaica, wife of Dr Robert Jackson in Jamaica, granted lands of Lumloch on 3 February 1818. [NAS.RGS.157.23.52]

CAMPBELL, THOMAS, merchant in Grenada, owner of the Betsy of Glasgow, 1793. [NAS.CE60.11.3/13]; died in Demerara on 14 May 1795. [EEC:23.7.1795]

CAMPBELL, WILLIAM, born in Stuckchapel, Glenfalloch, son of William Campbell and his wife Effie McNicol, on 16 November 1760, emigrated to the West Indies in 1778, a planter in Hanover parish, died there in October 1791, probate Jamaica, 8 June 1793. [SP.II.195]

CAMPBELL, WILLIAM, died in St Vincent on 7 June 1839. [SG#8/805]

CAMPBELL, WILLIAM, Captain of the 96th Regiment of Foot, youngest son of John Campbell of Lochend, died in Antigua on 23 October 1805. [EEC]

CAMPBELL, ..., son of Sir John Campbell of Ardnamurchan, was born in St Vincent on 27 January 1845. [PC#2010]

CAMPBELL, BLANE, and Company, merchants in Grenada, 1782. [NAS.CS17.1.1]

CARLYLE, WARRAND, born in Paisley, Renfrewshire, on 12 November 1796, fourth son of James Carlyle a craftsman there, matriculated at Glasgow University in 1810, a Presbyterian minister in Carlow from 1836 to 1842, then a missionary in Brownsville, Hanover, Jamaica, from 1843 to 1881, died there on 25 August 1881. [MAGU#251]

CARMICHAEL, STEWART, in Hanover, Jamaica, third son of Dr James Carmichael of Balinblae, granted the lands of Balinblae on 20 December 1800. [NAS.RGS.132.40.45]

CARMICHAEL, WILLIAM, a merchant from Glasgow, settled in Jamaica by 1750. [NAS.B10.15.7166]

CARNABY, THOMAS, a merchant, born 1 April 1780, son of William Carnaby, a merchant in Forres, Morayshire, and his wife Janet Courage, died at Montego Bay, Jamaica, on 10 July 1807. [DPCA#272][IJ:9.10.1807]

CARNOCHAN, JOHN, a merchant from Edinburgh, died in St Kitts on 2 December 1868. [S#7929]

CARNOCHAN, ..., son of John Carnochan, was born in St Kitts on 16 September 1867. [S#7553]

CARRICK, ROBERT, born in 1819, son of David and Jane Carrick, an engineer, applied to settle in Havana, Cuba, on 13 October 1857. [NAC.Cartas de Domocilio]

CATHCART, ANDREW, of Kingston, Jamaica, died in Rhode Island during 1792. [GCr#206]

CATHCART, JOHN, of Carbiston, died in Jamaica on 24 November 1791. [GCr#75]

CATHCART, WILLIAM, of Tower, late in Jamaica, granted lands of Kirkland of Kilmaurs on 2 June 1814. [NAS.RGS.149.22];1817, [NAS/RS54.GR1046/263]

CHALMERS, AGNES REID, widow of Alexander Scott Chalmers, died in Rutland Vale, St Vincent, on 23 February 1863. [AJ:25.3.1863]

CHALMERS, ALEXANDER SCOTT, born in Aberdeenshire, died in Rutland Vale, St Vincent, on 9 January 1863. [AJ:18.2.1863]

CHALMERS, ANN, Jamaica, married David Darling, a surgeon in Auchtermuchty, Fife, in the Canongate on 21 December 1798. [Canongate Marriage Register]

CHALMERS, JAMES, a merchant in Jamaica, 1765, brother of Ronald Chalmers a farmer in Dilduff, Donald Chalmers a merchant in Virginia, and John Chalmers a merchant in Glasgow. [NAS.CS16.1.125/13]

CHALMERS, WILLIAM, died in Dominica, 1811. [NAS.NRAS#3626/970][NAS.GD171/970]

CHALMERS, ..., a child of Hugh Chalmers in the West Indies, buried in St Nicholas churchyard, Aberdeen, 22 April 1782. [ACA]

CHAMBERLAIN, GEORGE, a divinity student in 1823, emigrated to Jamaica in 1826, died 1832. [AUPC]

CHAMBERS, CAROLINE DARRACOTT, eldest daughter of James Chambers a colonial revenue officer, died in Grenada on 1 August 1863. [S#2560]

CHAMBERS, HECTOR, son of James Chambers a solicitor in Edinburgh, died in Jamaica in October 1831. [ST.VII.490]

CHAPMAN, JAMES, in Nevis, 1776. [NLS.Acc.8793]

CHARNOCK, JOHN, in Jamaica, 1848. [NAS.RD5.811.558/562; 812.156]

CHIESLEY, WALTER, surgeon major on board the African Company's ship Rising Sun at Blewfields, Jamaica, 1707. [NAS.RD2.94.590]

CHILD, WILLIAM ARNDALE, Writer to the Signet, stipendiary magistrate of Tobago, eldest son of William Child of Glencorse, died in Tobago 20 October 1861. [S#1999]

CHISHOLM, JOHN, born in Ross-shire, soldier during the French and Indian Wars, then a merchant in Camden, South Carolina, a Loyalist, settled in Jamaica 1782. [NA.AO12.49.417, etc]

CHISHOLM, WILLIAM, in Jamaica, 6 August 1783. [NAS.RGS.121.286]

CHRISTIE, MARGARET, from New Cargen, Jamaica, died on 9 December 1862 in St Andrews, Fife. [S#2337]

CHRISTIE, THOMAS, in Antigua, 1759. [DA.Ogilvie.ms.p36]

CHRISTIE, THOMAS, in St Ann's, Jamaica, oath 15 February 1822 Moray [NAS.CC16.9.12, 312]

CHRISTIE, WILLIAM, late of Kingston, Jamaica, youngest son of Alexander Christie of Balchristie, Fife, died in Clifton on 5 July 1844. [FH]

CHRYSTIE, ..., daughter of William Chrystie, born in Kingston, Jamaica, on 11 October 1831. [PA#117]

CLACHAR, JOHN S., Jamaica, graduated MD from Edinburgh University in 1814. [EMG#49]

CLARK, GEORGE, born in 1833, son of William Clark and Elizabeth Fraser, died in Camp Savanna, Jamaica, on 21 May 1858. [Inverness Chapel Yard gravestone]

CLARK, THOMAS, born 27 September 1753 in Kirkgunzeon, son of Reverend William Clark and his wife Janet McKinnel, a physician in Kingston, Jamaica. [F.2.280]

CLEGHORN, LAURENCE, a surgeon in St Mary's, Jamaica, dead by 1757, brother of David Cleghorn a saddler in Kirkcaldy, Fife. [NAS.B41.7.7.216][NAS.GD237.18.10/8]

CLELAND, WILLIAM, in Martinique, 1729, son of Robert
Cleland of Pedenie and Jane Henderson.
[NAS.GD172.978]

CLERK, JAMES, Jamaica, Fellow of the Royal College of
Surgeons of Edinburgh in 1797, Fellow of the Royal
College of Physicians of Edinburgh in 1817, graduated
MD at Marischal College, Aberdeen, on 7 February
1817. [AUL]

CLERK, ROBERT, in Jamaica, 1741. [NAS.GD18.5329]

COCHRANE, ANDREW, late Governor of Dominica, died
1833. [NAS.GD172/644]

COCHRANE, JOHN, a surgeon in Jamaica, 1732.
[NAS.GD171.4209]; MD of St Andrews, applied to be
admitted to the Royal College of Surgeons in Edinburgh
in 1744. [NAS.NRAS.726]

COCHRANE, WILLIAM, a merchant in Glasgow then in
Jamaica, 1780. [NAS.CS16.1.179]

COCK, Dr WILLIAM HENRY, died in St Kitts on 20 June
1843. [EEC#20641]

COCKBURN, Reverend HENRY, minister of St Andrews,
Grenada, married Mary, daughter of Charles Ritchie a
merchant in Edinburgh, in Grenada on 22 August 1839.
[SG#8/813]

COCKBURN, Reverend HENRY, minister of the Presbyterian
church in St George's, Grenada, died there on 19 July
1854. [EEC#22622]

COCKBURN, JOHN, in Dominica, 1776. [NLS.Acc.8793]

COCKBURN, THOMAS, Jamaica, graduated MD at Glasgow
University in 1747. [GUL]

COCKBURN, WALTER, a planter on Mary Hill Estate,
Tobago,1836. [NA.T71/1572]

COCKBURN, Sir WILLIAM JAMES, in Jamaica, 1789.
[NAS.GD216.230]

COCKFIELD, THOMAS NELSON, born 1822, eldest son of
Edward Cockfield in Dunbar, a merchant in St Kitts, died
there on 27 October 1853. [EEC#22514]; testament
1869 Edinburgh. [NAS.SC70.1.142/861]

COLDSTREAM, ALEXANDER, manager of Mitcham Estate
in Dominica, eldest son of Alexander Coldstream in St
Andrews, Fife, 1799. [NAS.B65.5.8.104]

COLHOUN, ROBERT, in St Kitts, 1757. [NAS.GD237/12/47]

COLLIE, DAVID, born 1800, from Aberdeen, died in St Ann's,
Jamaica, on 6 March 1868. [AJ:15.4.1868]

COLQUHOUN, ROBERT, a merchant in St Kitts, 1729.
[NAS.B10.15.6183]; in 1757, [NAS.GD237.12.47/4]

COLQUHOUN, ROBERT, born in Antigua, eldest son of
Walter Colquhoun of Camstradden, matriculated at
Glasgow University in 1791, died before 1826.
[MAGU#165]

COLQUHOUN, WALTER, a merchant in Virginia now in
Jamaica, 1783, son of Margaret Williamson or
Colquhoun. [NAS.CS17.1.2/22,188]

COLQUHOUN, WILLIAM, born in Antigua, second son of
Walter Colquhoun of Camstradden, matriculated at
Glasgow University in 1793. [MAGU#171]

COLTART, WILLIAM, in Kingston, Jamaica, 1821.
[NAS.CS17.1.40/166]

CONNELL, JAMES, a merchant in Port Royal, Jamaica, was
admitted as a burgess and guilds-brother of Ayr on 17
June 1710. [ABR]

CONSTABLE, JAMES, born 1763 son of David Constable,
'28 years in Jamaica as a medical practitioner', died on
24 October 1821. [Dundee, Howff, Gravestone]

CONSTABLE, JOHN, in St Kitts, 1776. [NLS.Acc8793/40]

COOPER, HENRY, a merchant in St Croix, husband of Mrs
Henrietta Cooper sometime in St Kitts then in Inverness,
1795. [NAS.GD23.5.353]

COPLAND, JOHN, born in Ellon, Aberdeenshire, during 1812,
died in Tufton Hall, Grenada, on 16 May 1870.
[AJ:22.6.1870]

CORBETT, JANET, relict of John Balfour late merchant in
Glasgow then in Jamaica, granted lands of Kenmuir on
2 June 1813. [RGS#148/55]

CORBETT, WALTER, brother of John Corbett of Tollcross,
died in St Vincent on 4 September 1786.
[GM#IX.465.382]

CORRIE, THOMAS, a planter on Lower Quarter Estate,
Tobago, 1836. [NA.T71/1572]

COULTER, DAVID, son of William Coulter [1805-1875] and
Mary McBride [1810-1863], died Trinidad aged 34.
[Ballantrae gravestone]

COWIE, DAVID, born in 1826, son of Reverend William Cowie
in Cairney, Aberdeenshire, died in St Vincent on 8
January 1878. [AJ:26.1.1878]

CRAIG, JAMES, born in 1835, son of John Craig and Catherine Weir, died in the West Indies on 6 October 1876. [Bower gravestone, Caithness]

CRAWFORD, ALEXANDER, in Antigua 1753. [NAS.CS96/644]

CRAWFORD, DAVID, in St Eustatia, 1779. [NAS.CS16.1.175]

CRAWFORD, JOHN INNES, Jamaica, grandson of Charles Crawford of Kilbride, 1802. [NAS.RS.Dunbarton#1343]

CRAWFORD, JOHN R., 53 Lilybank Road, Glasgow, died on the Shirvan Estate, Tobago, on 28 July 1875. [EC#28366]

CRAWFORD, PATRICK, Provost Marshal of the Leeward Islands, brother of Hugh Crawford of Garrive, 1734. [NAS.GD94/216]

CRAWFORD, ROBERT, a merchant in St Kitts, 1783, partner in Crawford, Johnston and Company, St Kitts. [NAS.CS18.714.25]

CRAWFUIRD, JAMES GRAHAM, of Gartur, Stirlingshire, youngest son of Archibald Crawfuird, Writer to the Signet, died on Three Mile River Estate, Jamaica, on 9 May 1840. [W#54]

CRICHTON, JAMES B. M. M., second son of Charles J. M. M. Crichton of Rankeillor Mains, died in Jamaica on 29 July 1877. [EC#29978]

CRICHTON, WILLIAM, late in Jamaica, then in Dundee, brother of the late Thomas Crichton of Millhill, 1786. [NAS.NRAS.#3770, box 17, 812][DCA: H3453]

CRICHTON, WILLIAM, late in Jamaica, now in Balhousie, testament 28 October 1788 St Andrews

CROASDAILLE, EDWARD, third son of Richard Croasdaile a merchant in Jamaica, matriculated at Glasgow University in 1793, graduated MD from Edinburgh University in 1799. [MAGU#171]

CROMAR, JOHN, born in 1846, son of George Cromar (1799-1875) a mason in Aberdeen and Margaret Ann Johnston (1806=1879), an engineer on ss Edith Gorden, died at St Thomas or Curacao on 28 May 1879. [AJ:30.7.1879] [St Nicholas gravestone, Aberdeen]

CROOKS, RICHARD, Jamaica, graduated MD from Edinburgh University in 1793. [EMG#24]

CROOKS, WILLIAM, a planter on Belmont Estate, Tobago, 1836. [NA.T47/1572]

CROSBIE, WILLIAM, a Jacobite rebel, transported from Liverpool to Jamaica on the Elizabeth, master Daniel Cole, on 7 February 1748, landed 21 March 1748. [NA.T54/44]

CROSS, DAVID, of Glenduffhill, a merchant in Glasgow then in Jamaica, 1780. [NAS.CS16.1.177]

CRUICKSHANK, COSMO G., son of the late Dr Cruickshank of Haughs, Forgue, Aberdeenshire, died at Mount St George Estate, Tobago, on 31 August 1853. [AJ:12.10.1853]

CRUICKSHANK, JAMES, of Richmond, St Vincent, married Margaret Helen Gerard, youngest daughter of Dr Alexander Gerard, Professor of Divinity at King's College, Aberdeen, in Strathcathro, Angus, on 25 June 1792. [GCr#131]

CRUICKSHANK, JAMES, in Richmond, St Vincent, granted Langley Park on 20 December 1793. [NAS.RGS.127.111]

CRUICKSHANK, Hon. JOHN, born 1792, son of the late Dr Cruickshank of Haughs, Forgue, Aberdeenshire, member of the Council of Tobago, died there on 20 August 1850. [AJ:23.10.1850]

CRUICKSHANK, PATRICK, a planter in St Vincent, granted lands in Strathcathro, Angus, on 3 July 1782. [NAS.RGS.121.119]

CRUICKSHANK, SAMUEL, in Jamaica, 1780. [NAS.CS16.1.179]

CRUICKSHANK, WILLIAM, in Jamaica, died 1800. [NAS.NRAS#3328/3]

CUBBISON, CHARLES, born in Ayr, died on 2 August 1810 on passage from Jamaica. [GM.80.288]

CULLEN, ROBERT, in Antigua 1753. [NAS.CS96/644]

CUMMING, ALEXANDER, born 1766, estate owner in St Vincent, died there in September 1851. [St Vincent Death Register #92]

CUMMING, ANTHONY, born in 1799, died at Port of Spain, Trinidad, on 16 February 1861. [S#1805]

CUNNINGHAM, ANDREW, in Antigua, 1788. [NAS.GD21.632]

CUNNINGHAM, CHARLES, in Antigua, 1761. [DA.Ogilvie.msp56]

CUNNINGHAM, DANIEL, in St Kitts, son of late Robert Cunningham of Cayonne, St Kitts, 1745. [NAS.CS16.1.75]

CUNNINGHAM, JANE, a planter on Cradley Estate, Tobago, 1836. [NA.T71/1572]

CUNNINGHAM, JOHN, born in Kirknewton in 1738, married Mrs Elizabeth Westland, settled in Jamaica by 1762, father of James, Samuel and George, died on 27 September 1812 at Montego Bay. [St James gravestone, Montego Bay, Jamaica][Caribbeana.2.18]

CUNNINGHAM, JOHN, died on Cairncurran Estate, Westmoreland, Jamaica, on 21 May 1807. [DPCA#262]

CUNNINGHAM, ROBERT, planter in Montserrat and St Kitts 1715, 1733. [NAS.CS230/Misc.15/17][BM.Add.MS.18683]

CUNNINGHAM, ROBERT, a joiner, died at Cape St Francis, St Domingo, before 1734. [CM#2197]

CUNNINGHAM, ROBERT, Cayan, St Kitts, then in Leith, and Mary Gainer, former servant to Captain James Dalrymple, Process of Scandal, Commissariot of Edinburgh, 1740. [NAS]

CUNNINGHAM, ROBERT, a wright in Grenada, 1791. [NAS.RS54.30/209][NAS.RS81/14]

CUTHBERT, GEORGE, Provost Marshal of Jamaica, 1786. [NAS.RS38.PR15.10]

CUTHBERT, GEORGE, in Spanish Town, Jamaica, son of Lewis Cuthbert of Bogbain, Inverness, inventory 1807. [NAS.GD23.4.243]

CUTHBERT, LEWIS, from Castlehill, Inverness, acting Provost Marshal of Jamaica, 1790, settled at St Jago de la Vega, Jamaica, an assemblyman, died on Clifton Estate, Jamaica, on 28 October 1802. [GM.72.1162] [NAS.RS38.GR484/32][NAS.RD4.259/1303]

DALL, ALEXANDER CASTLES, born in Cupar, Fife, during 1817, of HM Customs in Falmouth, Jamaica, died there on 8 October 1840. [FH: 12.11.1840]

DALLAS, ROBERT, planter of 900 acres, St Andrew's parish, Jamaica, 1754. [NA.CO137/28]

DALLAS, ROBERT, a physician in Jamaica, dead by 1774. [NAS.CS16.1.157/282]

DALLAS, S. G., Secretary of the Presbyterian Institute, Kingston, Jamaica, 1814. [NAS.NRAS#333/1/5]

DALLAS, STEWART, a wright in Jamaica, dead by 1774. [NAS.CS16.1.157/282]

DALLAS, WILLIAM, late a millwright in Jamaica, then in London, 1774. [NAS.CS16.1.157/282]

DALLING, WILLIAM, a merchant in Jamaica, 1744. [NAS.RS.Edin#130/123]

DALMAHOY, JAMES, in Falmouth, Trelawney parish, Jamaica, dead by 1822, husband of Jane Christie, father of John Christie Dalmahoy. [NAS.CS17.1.41/611]; John Dalmahoy, son of ... Dalmahoy in Jamaica, was educated at the Edinburgh Academy from 1824 to 1825. [EAR]

DALRYMPLE, Colonel CAMPBELL, late Governor of Guadaloupe, granted lands of Gruigfoot on 3 July 1764. [NAS.RGS.107.119]

DALRYMPLE, DAVID, from St Kitts then in Methil, Fife, 1766. [NAS.SC20.36.12]; in St Kitts, granted lands of Ladifron on 23 February 1767. [NAS.RGS.109.160]; in St Kitts 1780, [NAS.CS16.1.179]

DALRYMPLE, JAMES, Balthazard Estate, Grenada, died 1851. [S.24.1.1852]

DALRYMPLE, WILLIAM, surgeon, son of late James Dalrymple in Fraserburgh, Aberdeenshire, died in Trelawney, Jamaica, on 31 March 1860. [AJ:9.5.1860]

DALZELL, AUGUSTUS EDWARD, Bermuda, graduated MD from Edinburgh University in 1812. [EMG#45]

DALZELL, Mrs ANN, in St Kitts, 1776. [NLS.Acc.8793/33]

DALZELL, GIBSON, son of Lieutenant General Robert Duff, husband of Frances Duff, a planter in Jamaica 1731, Depute Provost Marshal of Jamaica, 1739, probate 3 March 1755 PCC. [AUL.ms3175/2201,1; 2227,1]

DAUNEY, FRANCIS, educated at Marischal College, Aberdeen, 1737, a minister at St David's, Jamaica, 1784. [FPA#316]

DAVIDSON, GEORGE, of Lordsdale, a surgeon in the West Indies, 1779. [NAS.CS16.1.175]

DAVIDSON, GEORGE, a surgeon in St Vincent, 1784. [NAS.RS.Renfrew#1350]

DAVIDSON, JAMES, born 1843, second son of Mr Davidson, 14 London Street, Edinburgh, died in Havannah on 30 June 1862. [S#2230]

DAVIDSON, JAMES, a surgeon in Jamaica, testament 1869 Edinburgh. [NAS.SC70.1.141/876]

DAVISON, CRAWFORD, a planter on Anoes Vale Estate, Tobago, 1836. [NA.T71/1572]

DAWSON, WILLIAM, Jamaica, graduated MD from Edinburgh University in 1813. [EMG#46]

DEACON, CHARLES, Jacobite rebel, transported from London to Antigua on the <u>Prince George</u>, master James Nairn, on 14 January 1748, landed 16 March 1748. [NA.T53/44]

DEAN, ALEXANDER, in Antigua 1753. [NAS.CS96/644]

DE COCKBURN, GUILLAUME, born in St Domingo during 1762, an officer of the French Navy, formerly resident in Rochefort or Paris, moved to England in 1782, settled in Edinburgh by 1798. [ECA.SL115.2.1/2]

DEMPSTER, ALEXANDER, 7th son of James Dempster a surgeon in Cupar, Fife, died on Dunkley's Estate, Vere, Jamaica, on 24 October 1835. [FH:14.1.1836]

DEMPSTER, Dr ANTHONY, 4th son of James Dempster a surgeon in Cupar, Fife, died in Manchester, Jamaica, in September 1847. [FH:11.11.1847]

DEMPSTER, Dr DAVID THOMSON, 5th son of James Dempster a surgeon in Cupar, Fife, died in Spanish Town, Jamaica, on 3 December 1834. [FH:19.2.1835]

DENNISTOUN, ROBERT, from Glasgow, was admitted as a burgher of St Eustatia, DWI, on 16 September 1780. [NA.CO318.8.83V]

DEWAR, GEORGINA, daughter of Robert Dewar of Muirbank, married Reverend James Denniston, Montego Bay, Jamaica, on 10 October 1843. [SG.XI.1247]

DEWAR, JAMES, in Antigua 1757. [DA.Ogilvie pp/14]

DEWAR, MARY, daughter of Robert Dewar a merchant in Antigua, granted lands of Drumcross on 23 February 1768. [NAS.RGS.110/95]; 1778, [NAS.CS16.1.173/305]

DEWAR, ROBERT, a merchant in Antigua, 1768. [NAS.RS27.180.276]

DEWAR, ROBERT, died at Montego Bay, 15 July 1861. [S#1921]

DEWAR, WILLIAM, born in 1831, son of James and Ann Dewar, an engineer, applied to settle in Havana, Cuba, on 9 October 1857. [NAC.Cartas de Domocilio]

DEWER, ..., daughter of Plummer Dewer, was born at Montego Bay, Jamaica, on 20 January 1839. [SG#8/756]

DICK, DAVID, merchant in Kingston, Jamaica, co-owner of
the Mercury of Glasgow 1795. [NAS.CE60.11.4/21]; late
in Jamaica, granted the lands of Ellendonan on 20
December 1813. [NAS.RGS.148.46]

DICK, HUGH, of Mount George, son of Alexander Dick an
accountant in Edinburgh, died in Kingston, Jamaica,
1852. [S.14.4.1852]

DICK, ROBERT, a merchant in Trinidad, 1839.
[NAS.SC48.49.25.38/165]

DICK, THOMAS, a clerk in Antigua, testament 1867
Edinburgh. [NAS.SC70.1.134/704]

DICK, THOMAS, son of Thomas Dick [1813-1904] and Jan
McConnachie [1816-1898] in Ochiltree, died in Antigua
15 December 1886. [Patna gravestone, Ayrshire]

DICK, WILLIAM, born 1779, son of John Dick {1757-1833}
and Janet .....{1742-1828}, died in Jamaica during 1803.
[Bathgate, Kirkton, gravestone]

DICK, ..., son of Colin McKenzie Dick, was born in San
Fernando, Trinidad, on 16 May 1863. [S#2494]

DICK, ..., daughter of Colin McKenzie Dick, was born in
Ellerslie, Trinidad, on 6 October 1860. [S#1704]

DICK, ..., son of Colin McKenzie Dick, was born in San
Fernando, Trinidad, on 30 May 1867. [S#7459]

DICKIE, ADAM, born in 1852, died in the West Indies on 25
February 1872. [Sorn gravestone, Ayrshire]

DICKIE, JAMES, from Ayrshire, was admitted as a burgher of
St Eustatia, DWI, on 13 November 1780.
[NA.CO318.8.84]

DICKSON, JOHN, in Jamaica, 1762. [NAS.RS27.159.164]

DICKSON, JOHN, in Salem, Jamaica, 1778.
[NAS.CS16.1.173/287]

DICKSON, JOHN, of Hillhead, then in Jamaica, 1780.
[NAS.CS16.1.179]

DICKSON, JOHN, an attorney in Kingston, Jamaica, 1799,
son of John Dickson of Hillhead, Edinburgh.
[NAS.CS18.708.8]

DIGNUM, Dr HARRY GRAHAM, born 1838, died in Kingston,
Jamaica, on 24 January 1861. [S#1766]

DINGWALL, JOHN, on Salt Savannah Estate, Jamaica, 1856.
[NAS.SC48.49.25.56/239]

DIXON, HENRY, baptised 10 March 1786 in Gorbals,
Glasgow, son of William Dixon and his wife Janet Smith,

died in Cave Valley, Hanover parish, Jamaica, on 5 January 1801. [GM.71.371]

DODS, JOHN, an engineer in Trinidad, testament 1865 Edinburgh. [NAS.SC70.1.126/393]

DOIG, JAMES, in Antigua, 1753, [NAS.CS96/644]; will subscribed in Antigua on 30 July 1759. [NAS.NRAS.#0792/7/5]

DOIG, ROBERT, in Antigua 1757. [DA.Ogilvie pp/14]

DOIG, WILLIAM HENRY, in Antigua, granted the lands of Crookston on 23 February 1765; will dated 1765 [NAS.RGS.107.168][NAS.NRAS#0792/7/5]

DOLLAS, JOHN, son of John Dollas, a tailor in Jamaica, buried in St Nicholas churchyard, Aberdeen, 3 October 1754. [ACA]

DONALD, DAVID, in Jamaica, son of James Donald a merchant in Kirriemuir, Angus, 1777. [NAS.RS35.xxvi.116]

DONALD, JOHN, born 1839, a paper ruler, son of George Donald (1799-1849) a mason in Aberdeen, died in the West Indies on 7 May 1860.[St Peter's, Spittal, Aberdeen, gravestone]

DONALDSON, ALEXANDER, an atttorney, late of Grenada, died in Tobago 1852. [S.6.3.1852]

DONALDSON, COLIN, a clergyman, emigrated to Jamaica in 1801. [EMA#25]

DONALDSON or BLACK, SUSANNAH, in Jamaica, 1815. [NAS.RS.Burntisland.1.108]

DOUGAL, PHILIP, from 'in Schotland te Hemont', was admitted as a burgher of St Eustatia, DWI, on 8 August 1781. [NA.CO318.8.83]

DOUGLAS, ANNA CHARLOTTE MURRAY, wife of Henry Lowndes, died in St Thomas in the Vale, Jamaica, on 2 September 1853. [EEC#22494]

DOUGLAS, CAMPBELL, Jamaica, married Agnes Marshall, daughter of Robert Marshall a merchant in Glasgow, in Hamilton on 1 July 1793. [GM.63.670]

DOUGLAS, CHARLES JAMES SHOLTO, born after 1710, son of Sir John Douglas of Kelhead, Dumfries-shire, and Christian Cunningham, Customs Collector of Jamaica. [SP.VII.150]

DOUGLAS, JAMES, formerly in Jamaica, then in Wigtown, 23 November 1826. [NAS.MEP]

DOUGLAS, JAMES ROBERT, born 1825, youngest son of Archibald Douglas an advocate, died in Besquia, St Vincent, on 8 November 1849. [SG#18/1885]

DOUGLAS, JOHN, in Antigua 1713. [BM.Sloane#4065/121]

DOUGLAS, JOHN, in St Kitts, father of James Douglas who matriculated at Glasgow University in 1748. [MAGU]

DOUGLAS, ROBERT, in St Kitts, 1776. [NLS.Acc.8793]

DOUGLAS, ROBERT, late in Jamaica, now in Burntisland, Fife, husband of Janet Ross, 17 March 1848. [NAS.B9.8.1.166]

DOUGLAS, ROBERT, in Tobago, 1850. [NAS.RD5.842.62]

DOUGLAS, SAMUEL, a merchant in Jamaica, was admitted as a burgess and guildsbrother of Ayr on 4 April 1751. [ABR]

DOUGLAS, SAMUEL, merchant in Savannah, Georgia, Loyalist in 1776, settled in Jamaica by 1782. [NA.AO12/71/1]

DOUGLAS, W. R. KEITH, a planter on Buccero Estate, Tobago, 1836. [NA.T47/1572]

DOVE, JAMES, a merchant in Jamaica, married Jean Kirkcaldie, daughter of John Kirkcaldie a merchant in Inverkeithing, in Edinburgh on 1 March 1761. [Edinburgh Marriage Register]

DOW, EDWARD LESLIE, a surgeon, died in St John's, Antigua, on 30 August 1839. [SG#8/814]

DOW, JOHN, born 3 January 1760 in Ardrossan, Ayrshire, son of Reverend Robert Dow and his wife Janet Adie, a merchant in Jamaica. [F.3.79]

DOW, ..., planter on Dow's 60 acre estate, St Andrew's parish, Jamaica, 1754. [NA.CO137/28]

DOWNIE, ADELAIDE, daughter of Rev. Thomas Downie, late in Nova Scotia, died in Kingston, Jamaica, on 9 January 1867. [S#7350]

DRUMMOND, ROBERT, sometime in Jamaica then in Edinburgh, 1798. [NAS.RD4.264.460]

DRYSDALE, ..., son of James S. Drysdale, was born in Castries, St Lucia, on 14 January 1839. [SG#8/768]

DUFF, ANTIONETTE ALEXINA, wife of David Hutchison, late of Coffee Grove, Jamaica, died in Lockport, Niagara County, on 11 February 1860. [DC#23483][S#1476]

DUFF, WILLIAM, in New Providence, master of the Garland of Glasgow, 1801. [NAS.CE60.11.7/77]

DUNBAR, ALEXANDER, a merchant from Nairn, died in Kingston, Jamaica, during 1794. [GM.64.768]

DUNBAR, CHARLES, in Antigua, father of John Dunbar, 1778. [NAS.CS16.1.173/155][NAS.RS.Dumfries.XX.211]

DUNBAR, DAVID, born 1757, son of Patrick Dunbar a farmer [1724-1785] and Marion Dunshee [1721-1795], died on Rozelle Estate, Jamaica, 9 October 1786. [New Dailly gravestone, Ayrshire][NAS.NRAS#3572/40/20]

DUNBAR, GRACE, daughter of Charles Dunbar in Antigua, and spouse of John Hart counsellor at law there, 1779. [NAS.CS16.1.175]

DUNBAR, JOHN, a physician in Antigua, only son of Charles Dunbar in Antigua, 1779. [NAS.CS16.1.175]

DUNBAR, ROBERT, died at Orangehill, Jamaica, on 8 March 1829. [EEC#18322]

DUNBAR, STEPHEN, only son of Walter Dunbar in Forres, Morayshire, died on Eden Plantation, Jamaica, in September 1780. [Glasgow Mercury#III.381]

DUNBAR, THOMAS, in Antigua, 1770. [NAS.RS.Dumfries.XX.211]

DUNBAR, WILLIAM, in Antigua, 1759. [DA.Ogilvie pp33]

DUNCAN, ADAM, assistant surgeon of the 67th Regiment, son of Alexander Duncan a merchant in Aberdeen, died at St Joseph's, Trinidad, on 7 October 1838. [AJ#4745]

DUNCAN, ALEXANDER, in Jamaica, 1751. [NAS.RH15.69.2]

DUNCAN, ALEXANDER, a merchant in Jamaica, was admitted as a burgess of Edinburgh during 1758. [Edinburgh Burgess Roll]

DUNCAN, ANNIE, born in Glasgow on 10 March 1838, wife of Henry Leckie, died in St Thomas, Danish Virgin Islands, on 6 December 1864. [St Thomas gravestone]

DUNCAN, THOMAS, in Grenada, father of Thomas Duncan who was educated at Edinburgh Academy from 1824 to 1831, and Frank, born 13 April 1817, educated there also from 1825 to 1832. [EAR]

DUNCANSON, JAMES, son of Walter Duncanson town clerk of Dunbarton, died in Jamaica on 5 April 1797. [CM#11824][GM.67.528]

DUNDAS, ALEXANDER, died in Jamaica before February 1792. [GCr#70]

DUNLOP, ALEXANDER, a planter in Jamaica, 1782, son of professor Alexander Dunlop and Mary Leitch. [NAS.RS.Dunbarton#45]

DUNLOP, ALEXANDER, manager of the Colonial Bank at Montego Bay, Jamaica, 1843. [NAS.RS.Argyll#475]

DUNLOP, ROBERT BRUCE ELLIS, born 1844, sixth son of Henry Dunlop of Craigtoun, (1800-1867), and Alexina Rankin, (1806-1872), died in Kingston, Jamaica, in January 1877. [EC#28837][Dean gravestone, Edinburgh]

DUNLOP, WILLIAM, born 1775, son of David Dunlop [1739-1804] and Agnes Dickie [1742-1798], died in Grenada 1790. [Dundonald gravestone]

DUNN, WILLIAM, born in Scotland, settled in St Eustatia, DWI, a widower, married Sara Godet, widow of Henricus Benners, in St Eustatia on 14 November 1733. ['Afscriften huwelijksakten van St Eustatius van 1710-1750']

DURNO, JOHN, in Jamaica, 1809. [NAS.GD171.914]

DUTHIE, ALEXANDER, from Jamaica, buried 24 May 1765 in St Nicholas kirkyard, Aberdeen. [ACA]

DUTHIE, JAMES, sometime in Jamaica, died in Stirling during 1817. [S#17]

EASSON, GEORGE, an overseer in Jamaica, 1823. [NAS.SC48.49.25.19/242]

EASSON, JOHN, merchant in New Providence, Bahamas, owner of the Triton of Greenock, 1795; co-owner of the Mary of Glasgow, the Hannah of Glasgow, and the Glasgow of Glasgow,1799. [NAS/CE60.11.4/2; 6/1/83/87]

EASSON or OCHTERLONY, MARGARET, in Tophill, Little London, Westmoreland, Jamaica, 1880. [NAS.SC49.48.25.80/156]

ECCLES, GEORGE, merchant in Trinidad, co-owner of the Commerce of Glasgow, 1798, the Fame of Glasgow, 1802. [NAS.CE60.11.5/50; 7/13]

ECCLES, JAMES, merchant in Trinidad, co-owner of the Commerce of Glasgow, 1798, the Fame of Glasgow 1802. [NAS.CE60.11.5/50; 7/13]

ECCLES, ..., son of William Eccles, born on 27 March 1854 in Port of Spain, Trinidad. [EEC#22574]

EDGAR, ALEXANDER, of Netherhouse, formerly in Jamaica, 1747. [NAS.RD4.176/1/484]

EDGAR, ALEXANDER, late in Jamaica, then in Edinburgh, 1839. [NAS.RS.Inverness#841]

EDGAR, JAMES, a planter in St Mary's, Jamaica, 1779.
[NAS.CS16.1.174]

EDWARDS, MARY MACKENZIE, daughter of Alexander
Mackenzie Edwards and Mary Chambers, died in
Jamaica during 1875. [Dean gravestone, Edinburgh]

ELDER, PATRICK, a carpenter at Seven Rivers, St James
parish, Jamaica, in 1792. [NAS.RS.Perth#2767]

ELLIOT, JOHN, in St Kitts, 1776. [NLS.Acc.8793]

ELPHINSTONE, WILLIAM, in Jamaica, 1749. [NAS.RH4.70,
bundle 53]

ELRICK, ANDREW, a merchant in Jamaica, was admitted as
a burgess and guildsbrother of Ayr on 4 April 1751.
[ABR]

ERSKINE, DAVID, second son of John Erskine a gentleman
in Jamaica, educated at Glasgow University during
1793. [MAGU#170]

ERSKINE, JOHN, a planter in Jamaica, 1782.
[NAS.CS17.1.1/44]

ERSKINE, JOHN, in St James parish, Cornwall County,
Jamaica, probate 25 October 1786. [NAS.GD123/142]

ERSKINE, JOHN, a merchant from Greenock, died in
Kingston, Jamaica, on 17 September 1795. [GM.65.969]

ERSKINE, JOHN JAMES, Jamaica, graduated MD from
Edinburgh University in 1791. [EMG#23]

ESDAIL, JAMES, a merchant in Basseterre, St Kitts, 1778.
[NAS.CS16.1.173/322]

EWING, WILLIAM, in Antigua, 1760. [DA.Ogilvie.ms.p43]

EWING, WILLIAM, jr., a merchant in Glasgow, to New
Providence, 1800. [NAS.CS29.912.45]

FAIRBAIRN, THOMAS, in St Vincent, 1793,
[NAS.RS.Aberdeen#1172]

FAIRFULL, ALEXANDER S., from St Andrews, Fife, died in
Kingston, Jamaica, on 21 July 1852. [FH]

FAIRHOLM, THOMAS, a merchant in Edinburgh then in
Tobago, 1779. [NAS.CS16.1.175]

FAIRLEY, EDWARD, born 1825, second son of Edward
Fairley of the Royal Bank in Glasgow, died at Port of
Spain, Trinidad, on 24 February 1846. [AJ#5128]

FALCONER, COLIN, from Edinburgh, indentured servant on
Ninian Home's plantation in Grenada, 1794.
[NAS.GD267/5/32]

FALCONER, JOHN, in New Providence, Bahamas, a partner in William Ogilvy and Company, died by 1794. [AUL.ms3175/307]

FALCONER, ROBERT, late of Spanish Town, Jamaica, 1801. [NAS.PS3.CC16.9.10/88]

FALCONER, ROBERT, born 1821, youngest son of Mr Falconer in Silverhills, died in Trinidad on 4 May 1838. [AJ#4770]

FALCONER, WILLIAM, of Rosehill, Jamaica, 1845. [NAS.RS38.GR2272/262]

FALCONER, WILLIAM, in Spanish Town, Jamaica, lease 8 January 1808 Moray. [NAS.CC16.9.10,88]

FARQUHAR, ALEXANDER, son of Alexander Farquhar in Kintore, Aberdeenshire, educated at Marischal College, Aberdeen, around 1781, later in Antigua. [MCA.II.357]

FARQUHAR, ANDREW, of Alexander Barclay and Company, eldest son of Andrew Farquhar, Mains of Caskieben, Aberdeenshire, died in St Thomas in the East, Jamaica, on 2 October 1834. [AJ#4536]

FARQUHARSON, ANDREW, in Grenada, granted lands of Auchintoul on 3 February 1800. [NAS.RGS.131.93]

FARQUHARSON, CHARLES, Jamaica, graduated MD from Edinburgh University in 1806. [EMG#39]

FARQUHARSON, CHARLES, in Jamaica, father of Charles Miller Farquharson born 1815, educated at Edinburgh Academy from 1827 to 1831. [EAR]

FARQUHARSON, JAMES, of Invercauld, to Jamaica on the Rosamund from Greenock in February 1793. [NAS.NRAS#61/6/1]

FARQUHARSON, Major General JAMES ALEXANDER, of Oakley, Governor General of St Lucia, died there on 23 January 1834. [SG#3/232]

FARQUHARSON, JOHN, RN, born 1771, died in Jamaica on 30 January 1792. [GCr#93]

FARQUHARSON, JOHN, in Grenada, 1792. [NAS.NRAS#61/2/2]

FARQUHARSON, MATTHEW, St Elizabeth, Jamaica, died at the Rectory, Montego Bay, Jamaica, on 22 March 1840. [AJ#4819]

FENWICK, ANDREW, in Antigua, 1753. [NAS.CS96/645]

FERGUSON, ANDREW, MD, born 1813, son of Andrew Ferguson in Aberdeen, died in Kingston, Jamaica, on 30 August 1853. [AJ:5.10.1853]

FERGUSON, GEORGE, of Pitfour, a planter on Castara Estate, Tobago, 1836. [NA.T71/1572]

FERGUSON, HUGH, in Antigua 1757. [DA.Ogilvie pp/21]

FERGUSON, JAMES, of Middlehaugh, late of Jamaica, testament 1 June 1819 Dunkeld. [NAS.CC..8/160]

FERGUSON, JOHN, born 1784, died in Charlottetown, Grenada, on 21 November 1868. [S#7918]

FERGUSON, ROBERT, late of Manchester, Jamaica, second son of Thomas Ferguson, Young Street, Peebles, formerly of Leith, died in Howard House, Detroit, Michigan, on 12 September 1855. [EEC#322800]

FERGUSON, Dr THOMAS, eldest son of Reverend Ferguson of Inch, Wigtonshire, died in St Johns, Antigua, on 21 May 1845. [SG#14/1416]

FERGUSON, WILLIAM, a sugar refiner from Greenock, then a merchant in Mantanzas, Cuba, died there 16 August 1856, testament confirmed on 7 April 1865 Edinburgh

FERGUSON, ..., son of Alvan P. Ferguson, was born in Charlotte Town, Grenada, 4 July 1868. [S#7800]

FERRIER, JOHN, Jamaica, married Elizabeth Watson in Edinburgh on 29 March 1788. [Edinburgh Marriage Register]

FERRIER, ROBERT, a merchant, died in Nevis on 7 September 1839. [SG#8/812]

FERRIER, WILLIAM, a Jacobite rebel, transported from Liverpool to Jamaica on the <u>Elizabeth</u>, master Daniel Cole, on 7 February 1748, landed 21 March 1748. [NA.T53/44]

FERRIER, WILLIAM, a mason in Grenada 1805, [NAS.RS.Glasgow#5624]; then in Glasgow, 1810 [NAS.SC58.59.7.55]

FIDDES, ALEXANDER, born 1817, Fellow of the Royal College of Surgeons in Edinburgh, died in Kingston, Jamaica, 25 December 1869. [S#8273]

FIFE, WILLIAM, brother of Barclay Fife a merchant in Leith, died in Jamaica on 6 January 1810. [PC#63]

FINLAY, ALEXANDER, Lieutenant Colonel of the 3rd West Indian Regiment in Jamaica, then in Nairn, 1851. [NAS.RS.Nairn.6.17]

FINLAY, JAMES, a merchant from Glasgow, in Jamaica 1790. [NAS.AC7/64]

FINLAY, JOHN, in Jamaica, 1794, brother of William Finlay of Moss. [NAS.GD461.147]

FISHER, JAMES, in Jamaica, 1782. [NAS.CS17.1.1/46]
FISHER, JAMES DICKSON, only son of James Fisher a
    settler in Jamaica, matriculated at Glasgow University in
    1793. [MAGU#172]
FISHER, JOHN, youngest son of Charles Fisher SSC in
    Edinburgh, died in Irwin, Jamaica, on 14 March 1879.
    [EC#29503]
FLETCHER, ANTHONY, in Antigua 1753. [NAS.CS96/644]
FOGO, DAVID, in Antigua 1753. [NAS.CS96/644]; in Antigua,
    1759. [DA.Ogilvie.ms.p34]
FORBES, ANTONY GEORGE, St Kitts, graduated MD from
    Edinburgh University in 1788. [EMG#21]
FORBES, CHARLOTTE MARGARET, born 1848, daughter of
    James Forbes, HM Consul, died in St Jago de Cuba on
    12 May 1851. [EEC#22141]
FORBES, DUNCAN, died in Grenada on 10 November 1791.
    [Glasgow Courier#63]
FORBES, Reverend DUNCAN, in Little London,
    Westmoreland, Jamaica, 1875. [NAS.RS.Dysart.5.269]
FORBES, GEORGE, died in Grenada 1802.
    [NAS.NRAS#3626/757]
FORBES, JAMES, in St Croix, testament 6 March 1810
    Moray. [NAS.CC16.9.10, 271]
FORBES, JAMES, born 3 May 1851 in St Jago de Cuba, son
    of James Forbes, HM Consul. [EEC#22141]
FORBES, JOSEPH, a wright from Antigua, buried in St
    Nicholas churchyard, Aberdeen, 4 January 1764. [ACA]
FORBES, PATRICK, only son of Patrick Forbes a merchant in
    Grenada, matriculated at Glasgow University in 1811.
    [MAGU#260]
FORBES, WILLIAM, in Vengeance, Prince Rupert Bay,
    Dominica, 1798, nephew of William Forbes of Callander.
    [NAS.RH1.2.808]
FORBES, WILLIAM, a physician from Callendar, Perthshire,
    settled in Port Royal, Jamaica, before 1809.
    [NAS.RH1.2.796]
FORBES-LEITH, RALPH, MD, son of the late George
    Forbes-Leith of Knock, Aberdeenshire, died in Carriacou
    on 22 August 1868. [AJ:4.11.1868]
FORDYCE, EMILIA, daughter of Alexander Fordyce, married
    John Stennet, a physician in St James parish, Jamaica,
    in Edinburgh during March 1791, died in Jamaica during
    March 1803. [DF

FORRESTER, JOHN, planter in Jamaica, relict Elizabeth
Somerville 1750. [NAS.RH18.3.278]

FORSYTH, JAMES, a printer in Jamaica, was admitted as a
burgess and guildsbrother of Ayr on 4 April 1751. [ABR]

FORSYTH, JOHN ALEXANDER, born 25 February 1770, son
of Reverend William Forsyth and Margaret Turner in the
parish of Aboyne and Glentanar, Aberdeenshire, died in
Jamaica on 20 February 1800. [F.6.78]

FORSYTH, JOSEPH, Jamaica, graduated MD from
Edinburgh University in 1814. [EMG#47]

FORSYTH, WILLIAM, from Huntly, Aberdeenshire, died in
Trinidad on 4 January 1851. [AJ#5374]

FORTUNE, JOHN, in Grenada, 1848. [NAS.RD5.819.58]

FOTHERINGHAM, Dr GEORGE, a physician in Jamaica,
1772. [NAS.CS16.1.151/57]

FOWLER, JAMES, formerly of Jamaica, now of Easter
Raddery, Rosemarkie, Tain, Ross-shire, 1829.
[NAS.CS17.1.46/384]

FOWLER, JAMES, son of Reeves Fowler MD in New
Providence, died at the Florida Settlement, Falmouth,
Jamaica, on 18 March 1840. [EEC#20053]

FOWLER, JOHN, in Trelawney, Jamaica, father of Sarah
Williams Fowler wife of Lieutenant George Budge of the
Ross-shire Militia, 1816. [NAS.PS3.16.281]

FOWLER, REEVES, a physician in New Providence, Bahama
Islands, probate 6 June 1809 Bahamas,
[NAS.GD63/466]

FOWLIS, WILLIAM, in St Kitts, 1776. [NLS.Acc.8793]

FRASER, ALEXANDER, in Tobago, died 1784, will.
[NAS.GD23.10.594]

FRAZER, ALEXANDER, on St John's Island, Danish Virgin
Islands, 1841. [1841Census]

FRASER, ANDREW, son of John Fraser (1749-1802) a
weaver and Isabella Grant (1741-1799), died in the
West Indies. [Inverness Chapel Yard gravestone]

FRASER, DAVID, a merchant in Jamaica, 1771.
[NAS.RS27.192.342]

FRASER, DONALD, settled in Georgia 1768, Customs
Collector for Sunbury, Loyalist, settled in Jamaica in
1783. [NA.AO.12.109.140]

FRASER, HUGH, in Nairn, formerly in Spanish Town,
Jamaica, 25 December 1825. [NAS.RS.Nairn.2/36]

FRASER, JAMES, in Jamaica, 6 November 1798.
[NAS.SC20.33.13]

FRASER, JAMES, in Trelawney, Jamaica, died by 1823.
[NAS.G16.SEC/43.67]

FRASER, JAMES, born in 1832, son of William and Jenette,
an engineer, applied to settle in Havana, Cuba, on 10
February 1858. [NAC.Cartas de Domocilio]

FRASER, JAMES, youngest son of William Fraser a coach
proprietor in Edinburgh, died in Dominica on 29 July
1867. [S#7511]

FRASER, JANE, widow of Alexander Fraser in Dominica,
died at 6 Nelson Street, Edinburgh, on 29 February
1848. [EEC#21625]

FRASER, JOHN, from Inverness, was admitted as a burgher
of St Eustatia, DWI, 20 August 1780. [NA.CO318.8.83]

FRASER, JOHN, born 13 May 1789, son of Reverend John
Fraser and his wife Jane Smith, died in Jamaica on 16
November 1821. [F.1.255]

FRASER, Dr JOHN, eldest son of James Fraser in Glasgow,
died in Kingston, Jamaica, during 1794. [GM#64.768]

FRASER, LOUISA AMENAIDE, wife of Lionel Mordaunt
Fraser, Registrar of the Supreme Court of Trinidad, died
in Port of Spain, Trinidad, on 1 July 1879. [EC#29602]

FRASER, MARGARET, born 1827, from Aberdeen, died at
Montego Bay, Jamaica, in 1852. [AJ:16.6.1852]

FRASER, Dr THOMAS, in Antigua 1753. [NAS.CS96/645]

FRASER, THOMAS, born in 1824, third son of Thomas
Fraser and Jane Suter, died in Mandeville, Jamaica, on
2 June 1860. [S#1571][Inverness, Chapel Yard
gravestone]

FRASER, Dr WILLIAM, in Jamaica then in Edinburgh,
testament confirmed with the Commissary of Edinburgh
on 13 July 1769. [NAS]

FRASER, WILLIAM MACKINNEN, Antigua, graduated MD
from Edinburgh University in 1775. [EMG#12]

FRASER, WILLIAM, late a Captain of the Prince of Wales
Fencibles, died in Jamaica during June 1802.
[CM#121790]

FRASER, WILLIAM, son of John Fraser (1749-1802) a
weaver and Isabella Grant (1741-1799), died in the
West Indies. [Inverness Chapel Yard gravestone]

FRASER, ..., son of Andrew Fraser, was born in Grenada on
18 December 1876. [EC#28827]

FREW, FANNY, born 1823, daughter of Reverend J.M.Frew, Rector of St Thomas in the East, Jamaica, and Ann Bygraves, died in Kingston, Jamaica, on 24 March 1842. [GSP#718]

FREW, SOPHIA LOUISA, infant daughter of Reverend J.M.Frew, Rector of St Thomas in the East, Jamaica, died in Grenada on 24 February 1842. [GSP#718]

FRIGG, ANDREW, a shipmaster in Jamaica, son of John Frigg a merchant in Findhorn, Morayshire, 1780. [NAS.CS16.1.179]

FYFFE, CHARLES, youngest son of David Fyffe of Drumgeith, died in Jamaica on 15 October 1801. [CM#121847]

FYFFE, DAVID, in Jamaica, admitted as a burgess and guilds-brother of Glasgow on 11 August 1789. [GBR]

FYFFE, DAVID, from Dundee, a planter on Black River Estate, St Elizabeth parish, Jamaica, from 1761, returned home 1773; late of Jamaica, 1781, then in Drumgeight, Dundee. [NLJam.ms1655] [NAS.RS35.PR28/374][NAS.RS.Forfar.39]

FYFFE, ROBERT, son of Barclay Fyffe a merchant in Leith, died in Kingston, Jamaica, on 1 August 1794. [GM#64.958]

FYFFE, WILLIAM, in Westmoreland, Jamaica, 1799. [GA: T-ARD#13/1]

GAIRDNER, ALEXANDER, a planter on Adelphi Estate, Tobago, 1836. [NA.T71/1572]; died there 18 January 1849. [NAS.GD1.380.1.52]

GALBREATH, ARCHIBALD, a merchant in Savannah la Mar, Jamaica, 1801, [GA:T-ARD#13/1]

GALLIE, ALEXANDER, born 1839, second son of Thomas Gallie, East Linton, Haddington, died in Basseterre, St Kitts, on 16 November 1868. [S#7919]

GALLIE, ..., son of W. R. Gallie, was born in Port of Spain, Trinidad, on 15 May 1863. [S#2494]

GALLIE, ..., son of William Holmes Gallie, was born in Trinidad 28 May 1868. [S#7774]

GALLOWAY, JAMES, born 1758, '56 years in Jamaica', died in 1833. [Falmouth gravestone, Jamaica]

GALLY, THOMAS, late a writer in Edinburgh, then an attorney in Kingston, Jamaica, 1770. [NAS.CS16.1.141/343]

GAMMELL, ALBERT, born 1841, died in Spanish Town, Jamaica, 14 June 1868. [S#7795]

GARDEN, ALEXANDER, in Tobago, brother of Charles Garden a writer in Edinburgh, 1778. [NAS.CS16.1.174]

GARDINER, JAMES, in Jamaica, thereafter in Banff, testament 30 October 1820. [NAS.S.Aberdeen.I.W993]

GARDINER, JAMES, in St James, Cornwall, Jamaica, 1827. [NAS.SC48.49.25.23/97]

GARDINER, JOHN, a cooper from Port Glasgow then in the West Indies, 1817. [NAS.SC53.56.2/117]

GARDNER, ALEXANDER, late physician and surgeon in Westmoreland, Jamaica, 1788. [NAS.B59.38.6.6.184]

GARDNER, JOHN, eldest son of Alexander Gardner a jeweller in Edinburgh, was admitted as a Writer to the Signet on 21 December 1786, later an attorney in Jamaica, died in 1794. [HWS#76]

GARRANNAY, HENRY, born 1806, died in Observatory Cottage, Grenada, on 17 September 1868. [S#7879]

GARVIE, ISABEL, applied to settle in Havana, Cuba, on 25 May 1858. [NAC.Cartas de Domocilio]

GARVINE, EDWARD, a merchant in St Kitts, was admitted as a burgess and guilds-brother of Ayr on 3 October 1737. [ABR]

GAVIN, Dr HECTOR, medical inspector of West Indian colonies, 1851-1853. [NAS.GD112/61/3]

GAVIN, JAMES, eldest son of William Gavin a merchant in Jamaica, matriculated at Glasgow University in 1811. [MAGU#256]

GAVIN, THOMAS, a merchant in Grenada, 1809. [GA.T-ARD#13/1]

GEDDES, WILLIAM, born 1848, son of James Geddes a clogger in Lochmaben, Dumfries-shire, a plantation overseer in Tobago, died there on 14 August 1870. [AO]

GELLION, ARTHUR GEORGE, born in 1819, son of Thomas Gellion (1781-1840) and Helen McKinnon (1782-1829), died in Dominica in 25 April 1858. [Inverness Chapel Yard gravestone]

GIBB, ROBERT, born 1768, died in Kingston, Jamaica, on 1 January 1804. [CM#13032]

GIBBON, GEORGE, from Glasgow, died at St Anne's bay, Jamaica, in October 1800. [GM#70/1214]

GIBBS, DAVID WILLIAM, born 1815, agent for the Royal Mail Steam packet Co., died in Grenada on 28 June 1868. [S#7800]

GIBSON, DAVID, at Montego Bay, Jamaica, 1783. [NAS.CS17.1.2/233]

GIBSON, DAVID, in Jamaica, then in Edinburgh, 1821. [NAS.CS17.1.40/178]

GILCHRIST, GEORGE, a planter and millwright in Hanover, Jamaica, dead by 1777. [NAS.GD217.685]

GILLON, JOHN, late in Dominica, granted Wellhouse on 20 December 1805. [RGS#135/169/240]

GLAS, WILLIAM BRYCE, born 1806, sixth son of John Glas in Stirling, died on St Toolies Estate, Jamaica, 16 January 1825. [Blackwood's Magazine#XVII.760]

GLASGOW, ROBERT, of Mount Greenan, St Vincent, then in Mount Greenan, Irvine, Ayrshire, 1821. [NAS.CS17.1.40/274][nas.gd1/584/1]

GLASS, GEORGE, in Jamaica, then in Edinburgh, testament confirmed with the Commissariat of Edinburgh on 29 December 1796. [NAS]

GLASSFORD, ROBERT, a merchant in Glasgow, late in St Kitts, purchased Montreal Estate, Grenada, in 1761. [GA:T-MJ]

GLEAN, JAMES, born 1814, a colonial officer, died in Charlottetown, Grenada, on 10 August 1867. [S#7528]

GLOVER, CHRISTIAN YOUNG, wife of Reverend Duncan Forbes a United Presbyterian minister, died at St George's manse, Jamaica, on 23 May 1860. [S#1567]

GOLLAN, GILBERT, late of St Vincent, 1821. [NAS.CS17.1.40/198]

GOLLAN, ISABEL, widow of Gilbert Gollan, in St Vincent, 1813. [NAS.CS96.3571/3]; 1819, [NAS.RS.Inverness#1874]

GOODBRAND, ALEXANDER, a Jacobite rebel, transported from Liverpool to Jamaica on the Elizabeth, master Daniel Cole, on 7 February 1748, landed 21 March 1748. [NA.T53/44]

GORDON, ALBINIA, widow of William Gordon, stipendiary magistrate and Member of the Council of Tortula, died in St Kitts on 3 July 1840. [AJ#4834][W#66]

GORDON, ALEXANDER, in Belmont, Tobago, 1786, [NAS.RS38.PR15.15]; granted the lands of Pitlurg on 5

July 1794. [NAS.RGS.127.158]; in Tobago, 1800. [NAS.GD44.34.46.2]

GORDON, ALEXANDER, of Grafton Plantation, St Patrick's parish, Tobago, husband of Jane Margaret Morison, daughter of Alexander Morison of Bogrie, relict of James Ogilvie of Ascruivies, 1794. [NAS.NRAS#2971/120]

GORDON, ALEXANDER, of Cluny, a planter on Bacolet Estate, Tobago, 1836. [NA.T47/1572]

GORDON, CHARLES, son of Dr Charles Gordon in Jamaica, an apprentice in Edinburgh 1772. [Edinburgh Apprentice Register]

GORDON, CHARLES, a merchant in Jamaica, dead by 1773. [NAS.GD67/105]

GORDON, CHARLES, attorney and overseer of Albion Estate, St Mary's, Jamaica, died there on 27 February 1842. [SG#11/1080]

GORDON, GEORGE, a surgeon in Jamaica, husband of Elizabeth Denholm, 1753. [NAS.RS.27/142/349]

GORDON, GEORGE, MD in St Kitts, father of John Gordon, matriculated at Glasgow University in 1770, graduated MA, MD in 1775. [RGG#227]

GORDON, HANNAH, daughter of Francis Gordon in New York, late of Huntly, Aberdeenshire, died in St Kitts on 8 September 1862. [AJ:29.10.1862]

GORDON, HUGH, from Dominica, married Catherine Wilson, in MacDuff, Banffshire, on 27 October 1807. [DPCA]

GORDON, ISABELLA MARIA, in Spanish Town, Jamaica, 1850. [NAS.GD366/5]

GORDON, JAMES, a planter in St Kitts 1723-1730. [NAS.GD237/12/50]

GORDON, JAMES, a merchant in St Kitts, granted the lands of Tippersie on 23 February 1767. [NAS.RGS.109.165]

GORDON, JAMES, born 1793, son of George Gordon (1701-1764) and Elizabeth Irvine (1710-1766), died in Jamaica on 29 August 1811. [St Nicholas gravestone, Aberdeen]

GORDON, JANE CAROLINE, eldest daughter of George Gordon, married John Wallace Harris, Kingston, Jamaica, at George Island Estate, Jamaica, on 24 July 1834. [AJ#4522]

GORDON, JOHN, ['Jan Gording'], a widower, born in Scotland, settled on St Kitts, married Judith Markoe, daughter of Johannes Markoe and Maria Gerrits in St

Eustatia, there on 31 December 1735. [Afscriften
huwelijksakten van St Eustatius van 1710-1750]

GORDON, JOHN, MA, born on 17 March 1782 son of
Reverend Thomas Gordon and Elizabeth Michie in the
parish of Aboyne and Glen Tanar, Aberdeenshire,
educated at Marischal College, Aberdeen, graduated
MA during 1799, settled in Jamaica. [F.6.78]

GORDON, JOHN, a carpenter in Tobago, 1800.
[NAS.GD44.34.46.2]

GORDON, Sir JOHN, married Julia Gallimore, daughter of J.
Gallimore, at Water Valley, Jamaica, in December 1811.
[GM#81.585]

GORDON, JOHN, of Cluny, a planter on Bacolet Estate,
Tobago, 1836. [NA.T47/1572]

GORDON, JOHN, of Newton, a planter on Grafton and
Grange Estates,Tobago, 1836. [NA.T71/1572]

GORDON, ROBERT HOME, son of Dr John Gordon of
Greencastle, Jamaica, granted the lands of Embo on 3
February 1785. [NAS.RGS.123.108]

GORDON, THOMAS, of Port Maria Bay, Jamaica, son of
Reverend George William Algernon Gordon minister of
Keith, Banffshire, died at sea on 15 June 1807.
[DPCA#265]

GORDON, WILLIAM, Jamaica, admitted as a burgess of
Edinburgh during 1743. [Edinburgh Burgess Roll]

GORDON, WILLIAM, late of Tobago, 1816. [NAS.GD74/163]

GORDON, WILLIAM, in Jamaica, graduated MD in Aberdeen
on 23 November 1822, [AUL]; died on 18 September
1836 in the parish of St Andrew, Jamaica. [AJ#4639]

GORDON, WILLIAM, stipendiary magistrate and member of
the Council of Tortula, died in St Kitts on his way to
Tortula on 18 June 1840. [AJ#4832]

GOWANS, Dr JAMES, Belmont, Jamaica, 1807.
[NAS.GD417.211]

GRAEME, JOHN ALEXANDER, eldest son of Alexander
Graeme a gentleman in Jamaica, matriculated at
Glasgow University in 1789. [MAGU#157]

GRAHAM, ANNE CATHERINE, wife of David Littlejohn,
Kingston, Jamaica, 1796. [NAS.CS17.1.15/817]

GRAHAM, DUNCAN, MD, in Jamaica, married Elizabeth Kerr,
daughter of James Kerr a writer in Edinburgh, there on
10 March 1771, [Edinburgh Marriage Register]; 1774.
[NAS.RS27.216.215]

GRAHAM, GEORGE, son of John Graham, in Jamaica by 1765, a burgess of Stirling in 1768. [NAS.GD29.2054, 2167]

GRAHAM, JAMES, from Airth, Stirlingshire, settled in Jamaica by 1783. [NLS.MS#10925/5]

GRAHAM, JAMES, of Dougaldston, then in Grenada, 1776, [NLS.Acc.8793]; 1778. [NAS.CS16.1.173/157]

GRAHAM, JAMES, fourth son of Robert Burdon Graham of Feddel, Perthshire, educated at Glasgow University in 1788, died in Jamaica on 16 January 1806. [Caribbeana#4.17]

GRAHAM, JOHN, master of the Oxford, died in Jamaica, probate 12 March 1739 PCC. (3/38/34)

GRAHAM, JOHN, in Antigua 1757. [DA.Ogilvie pp/15]

GRAHAM, JOHN, in Grenada, 1776. [NLS.Acc8793/6]

GRAHAM, ROBERT, an estate overseer in Dominica, 1784. [NAS.GD22.2.67]

GRAHAM, THOMAS, of Buchlyvie, Receiver General of Jamaica, died 19 December 1763. [NAS.GD22.SEC.3/208]

GRAHAM, WALTER, died in Jamaica before 1785. [NAS.GD22.1.210]

GRAHAM, WILLIAM, a physician and surgeon in Westmoreland, Jamaica, admitted as a burgess of Dumfries on 20 August 1753. [NAS.GD1.403.71]; IN Westmoreland, Jamaica, 1757. [NAS.GD219.289]

GRAHAM, WILLIAM, a merchant, married Jessie Taylor, youngest daughter of John Taylor jr., a merchant in Glasgow, in San Fernando, Trinidad, on 24 October 1849. [SG#18/1878]

GRAHAM, ..., daughter of Cyril Clark Graham, was born in Government house, Grenada, on 9 December 1875. [EC#28502]

GRAHAM, ..., son of Lionel Graham, Assistant Commissary of the Ordnance Department, was born in Kingston, Jamaica, on12 September 1877. [EC#29022]

GRAINGER, Dr JAMES, in St Kitts, MD of Edinburgh, applied for admittance to the Royal College of Physicians of Edinburgh during 1763, [NAS.NRAS.726]; and his daughters Louisa, Agnes, and Ellen, in St Kitts, 1772. [NAS.CS16.1.151]

GRANT, ALEXANDER, to the West Indies in 1810.
[NAS.GD1.644.26]

GRANT, ALEXANDER, of Auchoyranie, residing in Jamaica,
granted lands of Edinville on 23 February 1765.
[NAS.RGS.108.212]

GRANT, ALEXANDER, in Jamaica, son of William Grant a
merchant in Kirkcaldy, testament confirmed with the
Commissariat of Edinburgh on 27 June 1789. [NAS]

GRANT, ALEXANDER, in St Croix, 1809. [NAS.GD23.6.459]

GRANT, ANDREW, in Grenada, 1779. [NAS.CS16.1.175]

GRANT, JAMES COLQUHOUN, Hanover, Jamaica, 1822.
[NAS.NRAS#0771/612]

GRANT, DANIEL, planter of 300 acre Maggotty estate, St
Andrew's parish, Jamaica, 1754. [NA.CO137/28]

GRANT, DAVID, Jamaica, graduated MD in Aberdeen 16
April 1764. [AUL]

GRANT, DUNCAN, in Antigua 1753. [NAS.CS96/644]; in
Antigua 1758. [DA.Ogilvie pp/28]; a planter in Antigua,
died on passage to Britain from Antigua on 26 April
1770. [SM.xxxii.342]

GRANT, FRANCIS, of Kilgraston, late in Jamaica, was
admitted as a burgess of Edinburgh on 29 July 1795.
[Edinburgh Burgess Register]

GRANT, GEORGE, son of John Grant a merchant in Leith, a
merchant in Jamaica in 1768, was admitted as a
burgess of Stirling on 23 August 1768.
[NAS.GD29.2167]

GRANT, GEORGE, in Jamaica, granted lands of Thornhill on
21 December 1795. [NAS.RGS.128.145]

GRANT, GEORGE W. N. C., born in 1815, son of the late
Major John Grant of Auchterblair, Aberdeenshire, died
at Lucky Hill Estate, St Mary, Jamaica, in 1834.
[AJ:4.2.1835]

GRANT, GEORGINA, fourth daughter of Alexander Grant,
died in Spot Valley, Penn, Jamaica, on 23 July 1877.
[EC#29979]

GRANT, HUMPHREY, in Antigua, 1753. [NAS.CS96/645]

GRANT, ISABELLA ELEANORA, daughter of Alexander
Grant of Tullochgrittan, married Major general Jervis
Grant, KCH, Governor of Trinidad, in Trinidad on 31 July
1842. [CM#17342]

GRANT, JAMES MACDOWAL, son of David Grant of Arntilly, Banff, educated at King's College, Aberdeen, in 1817, a planter in Jamaica. [KCA#2.431]

GRANT, JOHN, of Braggan, deceased by 1750, a planter in Grenada. [Aberdeen Sheriff Court, Warrants, 15.2.1771]

GRANT, JOHN, in Spanish Town, Jamaica, 1774. [NAS.GD248.61.2]

GRANT, JOHN, in Jamaica, was admitted as a burgess of Banff in 1775. [Banff Burgess Roll]

GRANT, JOHN, Chief Justice of Jamaica, granted lands of Kintullo on 3 July 1787. [NAS.RGS.124.166]

GRANT, LEWIS, on Magoty Estate, Jamaica, 1774. [NAS.GD248.51.2]

GRANT, PATRICK, in Antigua 1753. [NAS.CS96/644]

GRANT, RICHARD, in St Thomas in the East, Jamaica, 1776. [NLS.Acc.8793]

GRANT, SAMUEL, in Antigua 1753. [NAS.CS96/644]

GRANT, THOMAS, in St Vincent. [NAS.PS3.11.307]

GRANT, WILLIAM, of Glenbeg, a merchant planter in Grenada, father of Charles, 1778. [NAS.CS16.1.174]

GRANT, WILLIAM, son of Alexander Grant (1747-1805) and Mary Macintosh (1750-1812) in Fort Augustus, Inverness-shire, settled in Green (Island), Jamaica, by 1816. [Clach am Imbhir gravestone, Invermoriston, Inverness-shire]

GRANT, WILLIAM GORDON MACGREGOR, born in Grantown on Spey 3 April 1801, a planter in St Vincent, died in Edinburgh on 15 September 1849. [Dean gravestone, Edinburgh]

GRAY, ALEXANDER, of Garden Estate, Trinidad, died in London on 20 August 1860. [EEC#23529]

GRAY, CHARLES, a planter on Highlands Estate, Tobago, 1836. [NA.T71/1572]

GRAY, ROBERT, in Antigua 1757. [DA.Ogilvie pp/21]

GRAY, ROBERT, in Jamaica, 1773. [NAS.CS16.1.154/223]

GRAY, WILLIAM, of Iter Boreale, Jamaica, former Postmaster General of Jamaica , 1776. [NAS.RS3.360/436]

GRAY, WILLIAM, of Herboreal, late provost marshal of Jamaica, now in Skibo, Sutherland, 1782. [NAS.CS17.1.1]

GRAY, WILLIAM, born in 1832, son of William Gray and Catherine Scobby, an engineer, applied to settle in

Havana, Cuba, on 19 January 1858. [NAC.Cartas de Domocilio]

GRAY, WILLIAM, son of John Gray [1744-1794] and Jean White [1750-1817], died on Brimmershall Estate, St Mary's, Jamaica, 16 November 18…, aged 40. [West Linton gravestone, Peebles-shire]

GREENLEES, WILLIAM, a student, son of Matthew Greenlees a merchant in Campbeltown, died in Trinidad on 3 May 1842. [SG#11/1093]

GREGORY, ARTHUR, planter of 160 acres, St Andrew's parish, Jamaica, 1754. [NA.CO137/28]

GREIG, WILLIAM, planter of 6 acres, St Andrew's parish, Jamaica, 1754. [NA.CO137/28]

GUILD, WILLIAM, Jamaica, son of Provost John Guild, was admitted as a burgess of Dundee on 18 September 1817. [Dundee Burgess Roll]

GURLEY, ….., son of William Gurley of Peter's Hope, St Vincent, was born in Scarborough on 3 April 1825. [Blackwood's Magazine#XVII.759]

GUTHRIE, JAMES, died 10 July 1728. [Crosspath gravestone, Westmoreland, Jamaica]

GUTHRIE, JAMES, on Friendship Estate, Jamaica, 1801. [DCA: H2]

GUTHRIE, JOHN, born 1687, died 13 June 1739. [Crosspath gravestone, Westmoreland, Jamaica]

GUTHRIE, JOHN, in Grenada, co-owner of the Pomona of Glasgow and of the Alfred of Glasgow, 1798, [NAS.CE60.11.5/71/108]

GUTHRIE, JOHN, a merchant, late in Grenada, 1795. [NAS.GD18/275]

GUTHRIE, MOLLY, in Kingston, Jamaica, 1780. [NAS.CS16.1.177]

GUTHRIE, PATRICK, son of John Guthrie and Helen Yeaman [1740-1786], a merchant in Jamaica, died in 1821. ['The Guthrie Family', p.108, 1906]

HACKET, ALICIA, born 1824, eldest daughter of Dr Hacket, Deputy Inspector General, died in Jamaica on 17 January 1846. [PC#2008]

HADDOW, GAVIN, late a merchant in Jamaica, married Margaret Young, daughter of Young of Netherfield, in Edinburgh on 18 December 1763. [Edinburgh Marriage Register]

HAIG, WILLIAM, son of James Antony Haig and Barbara
Robertson, died in Martinique during 1794.
[Haig of Bemersyde pedigree]

HALDANE, DAVID, late of Turks Island and of Buccleugh
Street, Edinburgh, died in Grenada on 14 August 1838.
[SG#7/702]

HALIBURTON, GAVIN, planter of 130 acres, St Andrew's
parish, Jamaica, 1754. [NA.CO137/28]

HALL, JAMES H., in Jamaica, only son of John Hall of
Benacres, 1806. [NAS.CS17.1.19/294]

HALL, JAMES, late in Jamaica, married Mary Ross
Anderson,
daughter of James Anderson of Rispond, at Rispond,
Sutherland, on 13 September 1854. [EEC#22634]

HALL, ROBERT, a merchant from Glasgow, died in Trinidad
on 8 January 1820. [GAd#XIX/2378]

HALLIDAY, JOHN, in Antigua 1757. [DA.Ogilvie pp/17]

HALLIDAY, WILLIAM, in Antigua 1757. [DA.Ogilvie pp/17]

HALLY, JOHN, a planter in Grenada, 1854.
[NAS.SC48.49.25.54/67]

HAMILTON, ALEXANDER, at Morant Bay, Jamaica, 1776.
[NLS.Acc.8793]

HAMILTON, ALEXANDER WEST, appointed ADC to the
Governor of Jamaica, with the rank of Lieutenant
Colonel, 13 December 1800. [NAS.GD142/34]

HAMILTON, ANN, spouse of Austin Leigh minister of the
Gospel in Dominica, parents of Amelia, 1772.
[NAS.RS27.199.181]

HAMILTON, ARCHIBALD, in St Ann's parish, Jamaica, dead
by 1803.[NAS.AC7.76]

HAMILTON, CHARLES, a surgeon on Nevis, 1738.
[NAS.RD4.176/1.18]

HAMILTON, CHARLES, Collector at Montego Bay, Jamaica,
1769-1799. [NAS.GD237.9]
[NAS.NRAS#2177/1111][BL.Add.ms38218/293]

HAMILTON, GEORGE WILLIAM, son of John Hamilton and
his wife Helen Bogle, Northbank, Glasgow, settled as a
planter at Tulloch, St Thomas in the Vale, Jamaica,
before 1829. [NAS.RD5.398.536]

HAMILTON, Reverend JAMES, a planter on Whim Estate,
Tobago, 1836. [NA.T71/1572]

HAMILTON, JOHN, in Jamaica, was admitted as a burgess of
Edinburgh during 1735, [Edinburgh Burgess Roll]; in
Jamaica, 1736. [NAS.GD3.2.109]; testament confirmed
with the Commissariat of Edinburgh on 7 August 1786.
[NAS]

HAMILTON, JOHN, in Antigua 1753. [NAS.CS96/644]

HAMILTON, JOHN, born 1781, eldest son of John Hamilton,
a merchant in Glasgow, educated at Glasgow University
in 1793, died in Kingston, Jamaica, on 4 November
1801. [MAGU#172][GM#72/181][Caribeanna.4.17]

HAMILTON, JOHN, a planter on Risland and Indian Wall
Estates, Tobago, 1836. [NA.T71/1572]

HAMILTON, PATRICK, born 6 September 1757, son of John
Hamilton, died in Jamaica on 15 January 1788.
[F.3.458]

HAMILTON, PRIMROSE, daughter of John Hamilton in
Jamaica deceased, 1780. [NAS.CS16.1.179]

HAMILTON, ROBERT, in Grenada, 1776. [NLS.Acc8793/7]

HAMILTON, THOMAS, possibly from Kelso, in Kingston,
Jamaica, in 1807. [NAS.RD5.389.42]

HAMILTON, WILLIAM, born in June 1748, fourth son of
James Hamilton, a merchant in Edinburgh, and his wife
Helen Baillie, a merchant in Jamaica, married Elizabeth
Nisbet, died in Edinburgh on 15 December 1802.
[SP.II.55]

HANDYSIDE, R., born 1776, died in Jamaica 4 September
1796. [Greendykes gravestone]

HANNAY, WILLIAM, born 1791, died in St Vincent 1846.
[Glenluce gravestone]

HARRIS, ROBERT WILLIAM, Representative in Assembly for
St Thomas in the Vale, died in St Catherine's, Jamaica,
on 27 March 1830. [PA#45]

HARRISON-OLIPHANT, JOHN, in Jamaica, 1784, 1788.
[NAS.CS17.1.3/204; 7/19]

HART, JOHN, born in Girvan, settled in Jamaica, died in
1811. [NAS.GD2.252]

HARVEY, ROBERT, in Grenada, 1776. [NLS.Acc8793/1]

HARVEY, ..., daughter of Mr Harvey, born on 12 April 1838
at Deanery Park, Kingston, Jamaica. [AJ#4717]

HARVIE, ALEXANDER, in Barbados, 1746. [NAS.GD393/91]

HARVIE, ALEXANDER, born 1725 in Midmar, Aberdeenshire,
late of Antigua then in Aberdeen, 1760. [APB.2.204]

HARVIE, FRANCIS, of Antigua, died in Dominica on 29 January 1839. [SG#8/757]

HAY, ALEXANDER, merchant in Kingston, Jamaica, co-owner of the Commerce of Glasgow, 1793. [NAS.CE60.11.3/65]

HAY, ALEXANDER, born in 1807, son of George Hay, sometime farmer in Craigiebrae, Marnoch, then in Turriff, Aberdeenshire, died in Duckenfield Estate, Jamaica, on 3 August 1857. [AJ:9.9.1857]

HAY, BEATRIX, eldest daughter of Reverend James Hay minister in Roberton, Lanarkshire, wife of John Jamieson late planter in Jamaica, died in Portsoy, Banffshire, on 24 February 1845. [EEC#21157]

HAY, FRANCIS, born 1773, died in Jamaica 1811. [Dundonald gravestone]

HAY, JOHN WILSON, advocate late of Edinburgh, Puisne Judge in Grenada, died there on 27 May 1837. [CM#18297]

HAY, JOHN, son of A. Hay a japanner in Aberdeen, died in Low Ground Estate, Jamaica, on 21 June 1853. [AJ: 7.9.1853]

HAY, Captain LEWIS JAMES, youngest son of Lewis Hay in Edinburgh, a Magistrate in Port of Spain, Trinidad, died there on 9 September 1834. [AJ#4536]

HAY, MARGARET, in Tobago around 1847, sister of William Hay a shipmaster in Aberdeen. [NAS.PS3.16.52]

HAY, ROBERT, in Tobago around 1847, brother of William Hay a shipmaster in Aberdeen. [NAS.PS3.16.52]

HAY, PETER, born in Drumblade during 1777, resident in the West Indies for 69 years, died in Kingston, Jamaica, on 24 May 1869. [AJ:22.9.1869]

HAY, WILLIAM, in Jamaica, married Helen Innes, born 1752, eighth daughter of Alexander Innes, an advocate, and his wife Anne Rose, on 30 September 1784. [SAA

HEADRICK, Dr WILLIAM, fourth son of Reverend James Headrick in Dunnichen, Angus, died at Blue Hole Estate, Hanover, Jamaica, on 17 December 1848. [EEC#21784]

HEATH, BENJAMIN, a physician from Jamaica, married Marion Wallace, widow of John Galbreath a merchant in Glasgow, in Edinburgh on 3 November 1790. [Edinburgh Marriage Register]

HENDERSON, CHARLES, a planter in Jamaica, testament confirmed in 1864 Edinburgh. [NAS.SC70.1.13/641]

HENDERSON, CHRISTINE, or COSGROVE, in Spanish Town, Jamaica, 18 November 1839. [NAS.RS.Edinburgh.49/250]

HENDERSON, ELLEN ELIZABETH, born 1840, eldest daughter of George Henderson from Edinburgh, died in Kingston, Jamaica, on 9 February 1868. [S#7675]

HENDERSON, JAMES, a surgeon in Jamaica, testament confirmed with the Commissariat of Edinburgh on 2 January 1756. [NAS]

HENDERSON, JAMES, late of Grenada, a shipwright at Ladyburn, Greenock, 1809, then in Crawforddykes, Renfrewshire, 1810. [GA:T-ARD#13/1] [NAS.SC53.56.2/109]

HENDERSON, JOHN HALLY, son of Reverend John Henderson in Wanlockhead, of the Ordnance Office in Jamaica, died 3 October 1820. [F.3.329]

HENDERSON, THOMAS, son of Reverend Thomas Henderson and Rachel Kinnaird, surgeon of the 90th Regiment, died at the Siege of Havannah July 1762. [Skirling gravestone, Peebles-shire]

HENDERSON, ... son of W. F. Henderson, MD, born in Bath, St Thomas in the East, Jamaica, on 20 May 1847. [AJ#5194]

HENDERSON, Mrs, from Jamaica, was buried in St Nicholas churchyard, Aberdeen, 1 May 1788. [ACA]

HENDRIE, THOMAS SKINNER, born 1850, son of George Hendrie farmer [1814-1867 and Jane Skinner [1826-1860], died in Trinidad 2 April 1877. [Straiton gravestone, Ayrshire]

HENDRIE, WILLIAM, a planter on Carnbee Estate, Tobago, 1836. [NA.T71/1572]

HENDRY, PETER, died in Jamaica by 1768. [NAS.GD26.13.658]

HENRY, ALEXANDER, merchant in Kingston, Jamaica, co-owner of the Ariadne of Glasgow, 1799,the Commerce of Glasgow, and the Alexander of Glasgow,1794, the Swinger of Glasgow, 1800. [NAS.CE60.11.3; 6/59/106]

HENRY, JOHN, merchant in Jamaica, co-owner of the Flora of Greenock, 1801. [NAS.CE60.11.7/68]

HENRY, ROBERT, merchant in Kingston, Jamaica, co-owner of the Flora of Greenock, 1801, the Mary of Glasgow, 1803. [NAS.CE60.11.7/68, 8/27]

HEPBURN, PENELOPE, daughter of William Hepburn in Jamaica, married Arthur Law of Pittillock in Edinburgh on 24 November 1789. [Edinburgh Marriage Register]

HEPBURN, WILLIAM, born around 1712, son of John Hepburn of Urr, Dumfries-shire, and his wife Emilia Nisbet, apprenticed to George Langlands, a surgeon apothecary in Edinburgh, in 1724, later a surgeon in Jamaica, died at Dalskairth on 30 May 1775. [TDG#23/235]

HERD, JAMES, born in 1831, son of James and Ann Herd, an engineer, applied to settle in Havana, Cuba, on 10 January 1858. [NAC.Cartas de Domocilio]

HERRING, NATHANIEL, Jamaica, was admitted as a burgess of Glasgow in 1716. [Glasgow Burgess Roll]

HINCKSMAN, RICHARD, a merchant from Glasgow, died in Jamaica in June 1797. [GM#67/711]

HISLOP, LAWRENCE, jr., eldest son of John Hislop in Balwastie, Biggar, died on Leogan Estate, Montego Bay, Jamaica, on 16 April 1839. [SG#8/777]

HODGE, MICHAEL LOVELL, Antigua, graduated MD from Edinburgh University in 1795. [EMG#26]

HODGE, WILLIAM PACKWOOD, eldest son of Robert Hodge a merchant in St Eustatia, matriculated at the University of Glasgow in 1809, graduated MD from Edinburgh University in 1814. [MAGU#246][EMG#49]

HOGG, JAMES, born in 1823, Captain of the William, son of the late Captain John Hogg in Peterhead, Aberdeenshire, died in St Vincent on 6 October 1854. [AJ:27.12.1854]

HOGG, MARGARET, daughter of John Hogg an attorney in Jamaica, married Robert Primrose a surgeon, in Edinburgh on 10 November 1776. [Edinburgh Marriage Register]

HOGG, ..., son of A. G. Hogg, born in New Broughton, Manchester, Jamaica, on 26 December 1846. [AJ#5171]

HOLMES, JAMES, a merchant in Falmouth, Trelawney, County Cornwall, Jamaica, deceased, his widow Mary Ann Barker, and his father John Holmes a merchant in Greenock, 1820. [NAS.SC53.56.2/217]

HOME, ALEXANDER, in St Kitts, 1769. [NAS.RS.Berwick#15/371]

HOME, ALEXANDER, a merchant in St Kitts, 1782. [NAS.CS17.1.1/97]

HOME, FRANCIS, in Dominica, 1776. [NLS.Acc8793/3]

HOME, NINIAN, of Paxton, formerly in Grenada, 1766.
[NAS.RS.Berwick.15/227]

HOPKINS, JAMES, a planter in Jamaica later in Greenock,
1819. [NAS.RS.Argyll#2902]

HORN, JOHN, eldest son of John Horn a gentleman in
Grenada, matriculated at Glasgow University in 1793,
graduated MD from Edinburgh University in 1799.
[MAGU#171][EMG#30]

HORNE, JAMES CLUKIES, born 1848, fifth son of Alexander
Horne, 27 Buccleuch Street, Edinburgh, died in
Basseterre, St Kitts, on 23 October 1868. [S#7895]

HORSBURGH, Dr., in New Providence, 1759.
[NAS.CS96/1583]

HOSACK, MARY ANN, born 4 April 1810, wife of John Bell,
died in Woodstock, Jamaica, 28 September 1838.
[Girvan gravestone, Ayrshire]

HOUSTOUN, ALEXANDER, jr., in Grenada, 1776.
[NLS.Acc.8793/41]

HOUSTOUN, ANDREW, in Grenada, 1827.
[NAS.GD23.6.626]

HOUSTOUN, ROBERT, in St Kitts, 1776. [NLS.Acc8793/22]

HOUSTOUN, WILLIAM, in Kingston, Jamaica, 9 December
1730. [BM.Sloane#4051/141]

HOUSTOUN, WILLIAM, son of Allen Houstoun a teacher in
Glasgow, settled as a merchant in Jamaica, died there
on 15 October 1808. [GM#79.85]

HOUSTOUN, WILLIAM, Belmont, Grenada, Member in the
Assembly of Grenada for the parish of St Patrick, died in
Martinique on 2 May 1842. [SG.XI.1080]

HUDE, PATRICK, painter in St Kitts, deceased by 5
December 1749. [NAS.RD4.175.2]

HUGHES, WALTER, planter of 1200 acres, St Andrew's
parish, Jamaica, 1754. [NA.CO137/28]

HUIE, THOMAS, a merchant in Kingston, Jamaica, co-owner
of the Nancy of Glasgow, 1805. [NAS.CE60.11.8/63]

HUME, JOHN, naval surgeon, Port Royal, Jamaica, 1753.
[NAS.RS27.142.273]

HUME, ROBERT, youngest son of Alexander Hume of
Coldingham Law, died at Bagnals, St Mary's, Jamaica,
on 12 January 1804. [GM#74.596]

HUNTER, CHARLES, a merchant in St Kitts, graduated DL at
Glasgow University on 6 February 1766. [GUL]

HUNTER, JAMES, in Jamaica, testament confirmed with the Commissariat of Edinburgh on 26 February 1800. [NAS]

HUNTER, JOHN, a planter in Jamaica, married Eliza Mary Ballingall, daughter of Colonel Robert Ballingall in Canongate, Edinburgh, on 20 October 1794. [Canongate Marriage Register]

HUNTER, JOHN, born 1780, son of Robert Hunter [1745-1816], died in Kingston, Jamaica, 17 December 1799. [Inverkip gravestone, Renfrewshire]

HUNTER, JOHN, jr., a merchant in Trinidad, son of John Hunter, changekeeper in Marchtown, and Janet Marshall, 1818.[NAS.RD.Renfrew#14325]

HUNTER, ROBERT, in Antigua 1760. [DA.Ogilvie pp/30]

HUNTER, ROBERT, grandson of Professor Hunter of Edinburgh University, died in Jamaica on 1 January 1804. [CM#13033]

HUNTER, ROBERT, a cabinetmaker in Falmouth, Jamaica, now in Lochwinnoch, Renfrewshire, 1815. [NAS.SC58.59.6.23]

HUSBAND, JOHN, a surgeon in Antigua, 1744. [NAS.RD4.176/2/26]

HUTCHEON, JOHN, in Jamaica, will 23 June 1812. [NAS.CC16.9.10, 423]

HUTCHISON, GEORGE, in Jamaica, was admitted as a burgess and guilds-brother of Ayr on 30 April 1750. [ABR]

HUTCHISON, JOHN, a merchant, died in Trinidad on 18 February 1820. [GkAd#2393]; father of William Hutchison who was educated at Edinburgh Academy from 1824 to 1825. [EAR]

HUTTON, CHARLES, a merchant in Nevis, 1779. [NLS.MS#8794]

HYNDE, MAXWELL, in St Kitts, 1776. [NLS.Acc8793/28]

HYNDMAN, THOMAS, eldest son of Robert Hyndman a merchant in Antigua, matriculated at Glasgow University in 1806. [MAGU#218]

HYNDMAN, WILLIAM, from Greenock, a merchant in St Kitts, 1765, and in Grenada 1767. [NAS.RS81.7.414; RS81.8.373]

HYSLOP, MAXWELL, a merchant in New York, then in Kingston, Jamaica, 1809, son of William Hyslop of Lochend deceased. [NAS.CS17.1.28/400]

HYSLOP, WELLWOOD, a merchant in New York, then in Kingston, Jamaica, 1809, son of William Hyslop of Lochend deceased. [NAS.CS17.1.28/400]

INGLIS, ALEXANDER, rector of St Andrew's, Jamaica, NA. 15 July 1749 PCC

INGLIS, JAMES, a carpenter in St James parish, Cornwall County, Jamaica, NA. 24.9.1789 PCC

INGLIS, JOHN BALFOUR, born in 1839, youngest son of Andrew Inglis in Kirkcaldy, Fife, died at Cape Haiti, Haiti, in 1 January 1877. [EC#28808]

INGLIS, PATRICK, born in April 1701, third son of John Inglis of Langbyres, appointed the registrar of Chancery in Jamaica, died 1737. [Family of Inglis,p.10]

INGLIS, THOMAS, a merchant in Charleston, South Carolina, Loyalist, settled in Kingston, Jamaica, 1784. [NA.AO.12/52/249]

INGRAM, ARCHIBALD, Receiver General of Quit Rents, St Vincent, 1776. [NA.T1.513.206-207; T1.521.257-268]

INNES, ALEXANDER, surgeon in St Kitts, dead by 1779, husband of Frances ..... [NAS.CS16.1.175]

INNES, JOHN, planter of 1273 acres, St Andrew's parish, Jamaica, 1754. [NA.CO137/28]

IRVINE, CHARLES, in St Thomas in the East, Jamaica, 1776. [NLS.Acc.8793]

IRVINE, CHARLES, a sugar planter in Tobago, 1831. [NAS.CS96.1063]

IRVINE, RICHARD, in Antigua 1753. [NAS.CS96/644]

IRVINE, WILLIAM, from Leith then in Jamaica, 7 December 1810. [NAS.RS.Edinburgh.2/257]

IRVING, Dr JAMES, in Jamaica 1757, brother of John Irving of Bonshaw. [NAS.GD219/290]

JACK, EVAN, sr., in Antigua 1851. [NAS.RS.Argyll#140]

JACK, JAMES, Chatham Estate, Jamaica, dead by 1785. [NAS.GD23.6.441]

JACK, JAMES, a merchant in St Thomas Island, 1816. [NAS.SC58.6.28]

JACK, ..., daughter of Evan Jack in Antigua, was born in Helensburgh on 7 August 1839. [SG#8/793]

JACKSON, CHARLES, graduated MD from Glasgow University in 1767, a medical practitioner in the West Indies, later in Kelso. [RGG#288]

JACKSON, WILLIAM, St Vincent, graduated MD from Edinburgh University in 1794. [EMG#25]

JAMIESON, ELIZABETH, daughter of John Jamieson an estate overseer in Jamaica, married John Chirnside a farmer, in the Canongate on 15 July 1790. [Canongate Marriage Register]

JAMIESON, MARY JANE, wife of Dr Thomas Ross Jamieson, died in Kingston, Jamaica, on 15 December 1839. [AJ#4804]

JAMIESON, MARY WILSON, youngest daughter of Reverend John Jamieson, Methven, Perthshire, married William Milne, of Halifax Estate, Jamaica, by Reverend William Jameson, Presbyterian missionary in Goshen, at Lucky Hill Pen, St Mary's, Jamaica, on 16 April 1846. [AJ#5133]

JAMIESON, PETER, in Kingston, Jamaica, married Barbara French, daughter of John French, an advocate in Aberdeen, and his wife Christian Blackwell, in Aberdeen on 9 June 1796. [AJ]

JAMIESON, WILLIAM, a merchant in Jamaica, was admitted as a burgess and guildsbrother of Ayr on 4 April 1751. [ABR]

JARDINE, WALTER, born 1806, late of Jamaica, died in Lilliesleaf, Roxburghshire, 19 Sepember 1837. [Lilliesleaf gravestone]

JARVIS, THOMAS, son of Thomas Jarvis a merchant in Antigua, matriculated at Glasgow University in 1736, graduated MA in 1741. [RGG#292]

JOHNSON, ROBERT, eldest son of Joseph Johnson a writer in Edinburgh, died in Jamaica during 1816. [S#3]

JOHNSTON, ANDREW, planter of 308 acres White Hall Plantation, St Andrew's parish, Jamaica, 1754. [NA.CO137/28]

JOHNSTON, CATHERINE, second daughter of Robert Johnston of Annandale, Jamaica, died on passage from New York to St Ann's in August 1839.

JOHNSTON, DUNCAN, in St Catherine's, Middlesex, Jamaica, 1783. [NAS.CS17.1.3/373]

JOHNSTON, Lady GEORGINA COCHRANE, third daughter of the Earl of Hopetoun, and wife of Cochrane Johnstone the Governor of Dominica, died there in 1797. [EWJ#1]

JOHNSTON, JOHN, from Glasgow, was admitted as a burgher of St Eustatia, DWI, on 18 August 1780. [NA.CO318.8.83]

JOHNSTON, JOHN, a merchant in Jamaica, 1821. [NAS.CS17.1.40/180]

JOHNSTON, JOHN, of Maryfield Place, Edinburgh, and formerly in Kingston, Jamaica, died in Balcurvie, Fife, on 21 May 1829. [FH]

JOHNSTON, MARGARET, eldest daughter of Hugh Johnston, Bellevue Crescent, Edinburgh, wife of Archibald Scott, died on Thibou Estate, Antigua, on 29 September 1862. [S#2300]

JOHNSTON, MORRICE, son of the late James Johnston in Aberdeen, died in Kingston, Jamaica, on 17 April 1853. [AJ:25.5.1853]

JOHNSTON, ROBERT, of Annandale, Jamaica, died in St Ann's, Jamaica, in August 1839. [AJ#4789]

JOHNSTON, THOMAS, in Jamaica, 1817. [NAS.CS17.1.36/500]

JOHNSTON, WILLIAM, in Antigua 1753. [NAS.CS96/644]

JOPP, ALEXANDER, born 26 October 1764, son of James Jopp (1722-1794) and Jean Moir (1730-1782), educated at King's College, Aberdeen, in 1778, died in Kingston, Jamaica, on 26 January 1798. [St Nicholas gravestone, Aberdeen][KCA#2.351]

JOPP, ANDREW, in Jamaica, 1786. [NAS.RS8.PR30/128]

JOPP, DAVID, born in 1814, son of the late Andrew Jopp an advocate in Aberdeen, died in Manchester, Jamaica, in 1842. [AJ:2.11.1842]

JOPP, KEITH, merchant in Jamaica, co-owner of the Magnet of Glasgow, 1800. [NAS.CE60.11.6/18]

KAY, JOHN, a tailor in St Eustatia, dead by 1782, husband of Agnes Boyle. [NAS.CS17.1.1]

KEDSLIE, MARGARET, wife of John Gittens, died in Guadaloupe 1853. [S.14.1.1854]

KELLIE, MARTHA, wife of John Fisher, died in Bryan Castle, Rio Bueno, Jamaica, 27 June 1868. [S#7800]

KEMLO, W., MD, born 1795, surgeon of the 79th Regiment, died in Dominica during 1840. [S#24/2124]

KENNEDY, ANGUS, son of Daniel Kennedy in Glasgow, died in St Lucia during 1802. [GkAd#75]

KENNEDY, JEAN, married Robert Thomson, Jamaica, in Edinburgh on 30 December 1795. [Edinburgh Marriage Register]

KENNEDY, JONATHAN BROWN, born 1803, died in Jamaica on 4 December 1840. [Wigtown gravestone]

KENNEDY, ROBERT, a surgeon in St Eustatia, 1766. [NAS.CS16.1.125/72]

KENNY, ANDREW, St Croix, graduated MD from Edinburgh University in 1812. [EMG#45]

KERR, CHARLES, servant to John Hamilton a merchant in Kingston, Jamaica, was admitted as a burgess and guilds-brother of Ayr on 24 June 1735. [ABR]

KERR, DAVID, born 1845, eldest son of David Kerr, 21 Warriston Crescent, Edinburgh, and of Jamaica, lost at sea 23 December 1861 when bound for Jamaica on the brig <u>Columbus of Leith</u> in the Pentland Firth. [S#2065]

KERR, FRANCES ELIZABETH, infant daughter of Herbert J. Kerr, died on Kent Estate, Trelawney, Jamaica, on 2 November 1878. [EC#29385]

KERR, JAMES, a merchant in Antigua, was granted lands of Easter Grange on 3 July 1765. [NAS.RGS.108.34]; a merchant, late in Antigua, now of East Grange, representative of Kerr and Burles merchants in Antigua, 1772. [NAS.CS16.1.151/319]

KERR, JAMES, in Jamaica, admitted as a burgess and guilds-brother of Glasgow on 11 August 1779. [GBR]

KERR, JAMES, Jamaica, graduated MD from Edinburgh University in 1794. [EMG#25]

KERR, JOHN, born 30 November 1745 in Carmunnock son of Reverend John Kerr and his wife Susanna McGoun, settled in St Elizabeth, Jamaica. [F#3.380]

KERR, JOHN CHRISTOPHER, born in 1793, a farmer, applied to settle in Havana, Cuba, on 10 November 1818. [NAC.Cartas de Domocilio]

KERR, WILLIAM, Spring Garden, Jamaica, married Margaret Hunter, daughter of James Hunter of Frankfield, in Edinburgh on 18 October 1791. [Edinburgh Marriage Register]

KETTLES, WILLIAM, born 1794, died in Mantioneal, Jamaica, on 22 November 1836. [AJ#4649]

KIDSTONE, ALEXANDER, in Jamaica, 1850. [NAS.RD5.863.409/ 431/440]

KING, DAVID, in Forest Pen, Black River, Jamaica, 1880.
[NAS.SC48.49.25.80/155]

KING, JAMES, in Antigua, 1760. [DA.Ogilvie.ms.p43]

KING, JOHN, a merchant in Kingston, Jamaica, eldest son of
George King a merchant in Paisley, 1779.
[NAS.CS16.1.175]

KING, JOHN, in Sherwood Park, Tobago, 1820.
[NAS.SC58.59.8.39]

KING, WILLIAM, merchant in St Kitts, co-owner of the Polly of
Greenock, 1792. [NAS.CE60.11.3/54]

KINLOCH, GEORGE OLIPHANT, Grange Estate, Jamaica,
1770. [NAS.GD1.8.34-36]

KINLOCH, MARGARET, third daughter of George Kinloch in
Jamaica, married Thomas Kinnear, a writer in
Stonehaven, there on 4 May 1805. [CM#13053]

KIRK, ADAM, son of John Kirk in Kilmarnock, Ayrshire,
settled in St George's, Grenada, by 1811, married Sarah
Crooks from Kilmarnock in 1814, died in 1817.
[NAS.GD1.632.1-14]

KIRK, ROBERT, from Glasgow, a merchant in Grenada,
1853. [NAS.RS.Glasgow#3974]

KIRKPATRICK, WILLIAM, of Raeberry, late of St Kitts, 1775.
[NAS.CS16.1.1165/409]

KIRKWOOD, JAMES, Ensign of the 3rd West Indian
Regiment, son of Anderson Kirkwood in Glasgow, died
in Up Park Camp, Kingston, Jamaica, on 21 August
1868. [S#7843]

KNOX, ALEXANDER, died on Westerhall Estate, Grenada,
on 28 July 1843. [EEC#20654]

KNOX, HUGH, a Presbyterian minister in St Croix, awarded
an honorary Doctor of Divinity degree in Marischal
College, Aberdeen, on 25 November 1773, [AUL]; 1776.
[NLS.Acc8793/26]

KNOX, JOHN, late of New Providence, the Bahamas, died on
5 January 1810. [PC#52]

KNOX, PETER JOHN, son of Hugh Knox in St Croix,
educated at Marischal College, Aberdeen, 1777-1781.
[MCA.II.353]

LAING, JOHN, in Dominica, granted lands of Auchabers on 2
June 1808. [NAS.RGS.138.84.147]; Provost Marshal of
Dominica then in Surrey, England, 1821.
[NAS.CS17.1.40/256]

LAIRD, JAMES, Jamaica, graduated MD from Edinburgh University in 1803. [EMG#35]

LAMBERT, ..., son of Reverend George Lambert, was born in Arouca, Trinidad, on 21 June 1862. [S#2208]

LAMBERT, GEORGINA, infant daughter of Reverend George Lambert, died in San Fernando, Trinidad, on 24 August 1863. [S#2586]

LAMBIE, NEIL, in St Thomas in the East, Jamaica, 1776. [NLS.Acc.8793]

LAMBIE, WILLIAM, a planter in St Thomas in the East, Jamaica, before 1769. [NAS.B10.15.7303]

LAMBIE, WILLIAM, Jamaica, married Elizabeth Dundas Crichton, daughter of Patrick Crichton in Jamaica, in Edinburgh during 1820. [GM#90/563]

LAMONT, JOHN, of Benmore, resident of Cedar Grove, Trinidad, 1853. [NAS.RS.Argyll#680]

LANG, ALEXANDER MORRISON, medical practitioner in Kingston, Jamaica, 1888, brother of David Lang an advocate in Edinburgh who died 29 April 1886. [NAS.SH.19.6.1888]

LANG, HUGH, in Grenada, 1776. [NLS.Acc8793/8]

LANG, JESSIE MORRIS, youngest daughter of Robert Lang in Largs, Ayrshire, died in St Croix on 14 September 1842. [SG.XI.1080][GSP#779]

LANG, JOHN, of St Croix, resident in Blackdales, Largs, Ayrshire, was granted lands of Knockewart on 17 March 1851 [NAS.RGS/247/4/8]

LANG, MALCOLM, planter of 150 acres, St Andrew's parish, Jamaica, 1754. [NA.CO137/28]

LANG, ROBERT, planter, St Thomas in the East, Surrey County, Jamaica, 1789. [NAS.RS.Glasgow#1190]

LANGLANDS, DONALD, born 1776, son of George Langlands a land surveyor in Campbelltown, died in Trinidad during 1803. [CM#121866]

LAPSLEY, WILLIAM, born in St Kitts during only son of James Lapsley, matriculated at Glasgow University 1792. [MAGU#168]

LAUDER, GEORGE, of Pitscandly, a former merchant in Jamaica, dead by 1760. [NAS.B18.4.8.16]

LAURIE, JOHN, born 1787, son of James Laurie in Glasgow, died in Curacao on 10 July 1809. [PC#20]

LAW, WILLIAM, only son of Reverend John Law in
Innerleithen, died in Port of Spain, Trinidad, on 21
August 1855. [Fifeshire Express#9][EEC#322794]

LAWRENCE, WILLIAM, a missionary of the United
Presbyterian Church, died at Mount Zion, Cornwall,
Jamaica, on 17 November 1869. [S#8231]

LAWRIE, JAMES, in Port Antonio, Jamaica, 1740.
[NAS.GD461.21]

LAWSON, CHARLOTTE, widow of Reverend George Brodie,
died at the Presbyterian Manse, Port of Spain, Trinidad,
on 14 April 1876. [EC#28591]

LAWSON, GEORGE MCFARQUHAR, Jamaica, graduated
MD from Edinburgh University in 1788. [EMG#21]

LAWSON, WILSON, in Tortula, Virgin Islands, 1800.
[NAS.CS26.915.35]

LECKIE, JAMES, son of William Leckie of Brioch,
Stirlingshire, died in St James parish, Jamaica, on 24
August 1792. [GCr#188]

LECKIE, WILLIAM, a surgeon in Jamaica, married Janet
Buchanan, daughter of John Buchanan, in Edinburgh on
5 August 1753. [Edinburgh Marriage Register]

LEGGAT, JOHN, born 1797, died in St Thomas in the East,
Jamaica, 4 June 1816, son of William Leggat (1750-
1840) and Jane McDowall(1761-1843). [Glenluce
gravestone]

LEITCH, GEORGE, died in Nassau, New Providence, on 25
October 1809. [PC#46]

LEITCH, JOHN, from Glasgow, was admitted as a burgher of
St Eustatia on 8 August 1780. [NA.CO318.8.83]

LEITH, JOHN, at Annotto Bay, Jamaica, grandson of John
Leith of Blaur, 1790. [NAS.RS8.PR31/367]

LEITH, JOHN, in Kingston, Jamaica, testament confirmed on
4 August 1800 with the Commissariat of Edinburgh.
[NAS]

LEITH, JOHN, a sugar planter in Tobago, 1831.
[NAS.CS96.1063]

LEITH, RALPH FORBES, health officer, died in Bel Air
House, Carriacou, on 22 September 1868. [S#7855]

LENNOX or DONALDSON, JAMES, at Morant Bay, Jamaica,
1821. [NAS.SC48.49.25.17/26]

LENNOX, JAMES, born 1790, a surgeon in Jamaica, died 15
September 1814. [Rhu gravestone]

LEONARD, GEORGE, a student at Marischal College, Aberdeen, 1770-1774, son of George Leonard of Salt River, Jamaica. [MCA.II.341]

LESLIE, ANDREW, in Antigua 1753. [NAS.CS96/644]

LESLIE, ANDREW, in Tortula, Virgin Islands, 1800. [NAS.CS26.915.35]

LESLIE, THOMAS, of the brig <u>Princess of Wales of Leith</u>, died in Jamaica on 6 February 1797. [CM#11803]

LESLIE, WILLIAM, in Antigua, 1760. [DA.Ogilvie pp32]

LEWIS, JAMES, son of James Lewis a gentleman in Spanish Town, Jamaica, matriculated at Glasgow University in 1793. [MAGU#173]

LIGERTWOOD, CHRISTIAN, daughter of Alexander Ligertwood in St Vincent, married James Ross from Leith, in Aberdeen on 20 October 1874. [SC#27097]

LINDSAY, GEORGE, born 6 February 1737, a writer or lawyer, died at Savannah 9 September 1762. [SP.V.417]

LINDSAY, JAMES, only son of James Lindsay a merchant in Tobago, matriculated at Glasgow University in 1807. [MAGU#232]

LINDSAY, JOHN, Rector of St Thomas, Jamaica, graduated DD at Glasgow University on 12 January 1773. [GUL]

LITHGOW, THOMAS, a planter in Grenada, 1779. [NAS.CS16.1.175]

LITTLE, ARCHIBALD, born 22 December 1782, son of Reverend James Little and his wife Elizabeth Clarke, died in Jamaica on 16 February 1804. [F#2.262]

LITTLE, GEORGE, MA, died in Jamaica before February 1792. [GCr#70]

LITTLEJOHN, DAVID, born 1744, late of Jamaica, died in Edinburgh on 2 August 1833. [SG#2/167]

LITTLEJOHN, JAMES, son of Peter Littlejohn at Mains of Hazlehead, Aberdeen, died in Guadaloupe, 1760. [APB.2.215]

LIVINGSTONE, WILLIAM, in Antigua 1757. [DA.Ogilvie pp/19]

LLOYD, REBECCA M. E., died 5 September 1850 on Riviere Doree Estate, St Lucia. [EEC#22057]

LOCH, WILLIAM, fourth son of William Loch (1709-1779) and his wife Margaret Brown, Hawkshaw, Kirkcudbright, settled in Jamaica. [Family of Loch, p.425, Edinburgh, 1934]

LOGAN, JAMES, chairman of the Quarter Sessions for Hanover and Westmoreland, Jamaica, brother of George Logan of Edrom, 1842, in Jamaica 1844. [NAS.GD1.384.8/14]

LOGAN, THOMAS, born 1772, late of Jamaica, died 13 September 1831. [Straiton gravestone, Ayrshire]

LOVE, ALLAN, from Greenock, a mariner in Montserrat, 1778. [NAS.RS81/10]

LOW, ELIZA CARTWRIGHT, youngest daughter of Rev. William Low in Portobello, Midlothian, wife of Rev. Augustus Sullivan minister of San Salvador, died in Arthur Town, San Salvador, Bahamas, on 9 December 1866. [S#7312]

LUMSDEN, ALEXANDER, born in Aberdeen during 1751, died in Grenada on 12 May 1838. [SG#7/684]

LUMSDEN, ALEXANDER, born 20 June 1786 in Aberdeen, fourth son of Harry Lumsden and his wife Catherine McVeagh, settled in St Dorothy, Jamaica, died 1 September 1826. [SAA

LUMSDEN, HENRY, son of William Lumsden and his wife Rachel in Mid Clova, Kildrummy, Balmedie, Aberdeenshire, a cooper who emigrated to Jamaica in 1760, died in Aberdeen during April 1796. [TOF#628]

LUMSDEN, JAMES, born 1770, late of Jamaica, died in Aberdeen on 9 May 1834. [ANQ.3.29]

LUNDIE, WALTER, born 28 March 1750 in Erskine, Renfrewshire, son of Reverend James Lundie and his wife Christian Ballantyne, a physician in Jamaica. [F.3.193]

LYALL, JAMES GIBSON, of Gallery, late in Jamaica, only son of James Gibson Lyall, granted the lands of Gallery on 1 June 1816. [NAS.RGS.154.17]

LYNCH, MARY A., in Clarendon, Jamaica, 7 September 1824. [NAS.RS.Edinburgh.24/178]

LYON, DAVID, ('David Lijens'), bachelor, mariner, born in Scotland, married Rebecca Davids, widow of Jan Schoot, on 27 December 1736. ['Afscriften huwelijksakten van St Eustatius van 1710-1750']

LYON, ELIZABETH, daughter of James Lyon a wright in Jamaica, married William Turnbull a gentleman's servant, in Edinburgh on 15 June 1785. [Edinburgh Marriage Register]

LYON, WILLIAM, in Grenada, 1794.
[NAS.RS.Glasgow#6002]

LYON, WILLIAM, in St Kitts, 1776. [NLS.Acc.8793/37]

MACK, THOMAS, in Kingston, Jamaica, 1786 to 1795, later
tenant in Gordon Mains, Berwickshire, 1800.
[NAS.CS26.912.14]

MCALISTER, ALEXANDER, a planter in Dominica, 1776.
[NA.T1.520.3-4]

MCALLAN, WALTER, from Perthshire, was admitted as a
burgher of St Eustatia, DWI, on 9 August 1780.
[NA.CO318.8.83]

MCALPINE, GREGORY, in Antigua, 1754. [NAS.CS96/647]

MCANDREW, GEORGE SHIRLEY, son of James McAndrew
a merchant in Elgin, educated at King's College,
Aberdeen, in 1812, settled in Jamaica. [KCA.2.414]

MCARTHUR, DUNCAN, in St Vincent, 1816.
[NAS.SC53.56.2/130]; in St Vincent, 1820,
[NAS.RS.Argyll#3149]; merchant in St Vincent, now in
Glasgow 1837. [NAS.SC58.59.15.1]; late of St Vincent,
deceased by 1842. [NAS.RS.Argyll#168]

MCARTHUR, HELEN, in St Vincent, 1838.
[NAS.SC58.42.11.126]

MCARTHUR, JOHN MELVIL, in St Vincent, 1842.
[NAS.RS.Argyll#168]

MCBARNET, ALEXANDER, in St Vincent, granted the lands
of Attadale on 21 December 1840. [NAS.RGS.223.4]

MCBEAN, ANGUS, a merchant in Kingston, Jamaica, 1778.
[NAS.CS16.1.173/34]

MCBEAN, JAMES A. D., staff surgeon, eldest son of
Lieutenant Colonel James McBean of the 78th
Highlanders, died in Lucea, Jamaica, on 17 January
1853. [EEC#22405]

MCBEAN, JOHN, late of Jamaica, died in Brompton on 22
September 1834. [AJ#4525]

MCBEAN, ROBERT, late of Tortula, Virgin Islands, 1798,
1802. [NAS.RS38.PR16/389][NAS.GD23.4.234]

MCBEATH, GEORGE, in Trinidad, co-owner of the Garland of
Glasgow, 1801. [NAS.CE60.11.7/77]

MCCALLUM, ALEXANDER, in Lucca, Jamaica, 1818.
[NAS.RS.Argyll#2860]

MCCALLUM, DAVID, in Antigua 1753. [NAS.CS96/644]

MCCALLUM, NEIL, planter in Hanover parish, Jamaica,
1828, [NAS.RS.Argyll#126];1836. [NAS.GD1.35V, 29]

MCCALMAN, DUNCAN, son of Dr McCalman in Islay, Argyll, died in Jamaica during March 1795. [GM.65.791]

MCCAUL, JOHN, merchant in Kingston, Jamaica, co-owner of the <u>Mercury of Glasgow</u> 1795. [NAS.CE60.11.4/21]

MCCAUL, JOHN, second son of Gilbert McCaul in Glasgow, a merchant who died in Antigua on 17 April 1830. [PA#45]

MCCAUL, JOHN GORDON, son of John McCaul a merchant in Glasgow, a merchant in St Croix, 1821. [NAS.CS17.1.40/571]

MCCLYMONT, JAMES, son of James McClymont [1745-1825], died in Jamaica in September 1810. [Straiton gravestone, Ayrshire]

MCCOLL, JAMES, from Glasgow then in New York now in the West Indies, 1787, 1788. [NAS.CS17.1.6/198; 7/17]

MCCOLL, JOHN, of Betsy's Hope, died in Scarborough, Tobago, on 24 March 1879. [EC#29503]

MCCOM, BENJAMIN, in Antigua 1753. [NAS.CS96/644]

MCCOMBIE, ALEXANDER, born in 1786, from Aberdeen, emigrated in 1806, died in St Lucia on 22 April 1865. [AJ:7.6.1865]

MCCOMBIE, ALEXANDER, jr., eldest son of Alexander McCombie in St Lucia, married Ella, youngest daughter of Michael Cooke, Palatine House, County Carlow, at Trinity Church, Castries, St Lucia, on 20 March 1851. [AJ#5390]

MCCOMBIE, GEORGE, born 1832, son of Alexander McCombie in St Lucia, died at 11 North Broadford, Aberdeen, on 19 September 1851. [AJ#5411]

MCCOMBIE, JOHN ROSS, married Margaret, eldest daughter of late William Swap, at Calviny Cottage, Grenada, on 2 November 1840. [AJ#4854]

MCCOOK, FRANCIS, born in Old Meldrum, Aberdeenshire, during 1790, died in Kingston, Jamaica, on 17 November 1850. [AJ:1.1.1851]

MCCOOK, JOHN, born 13 September 1797, son of James McCook and his wife Isabella Kynoch in Aberdeen, educated at Marischal College, Aberdeen, in 1814, a planter in Jamaica, died there on 20 September 1829. [SAA

MCCORMICK, JOHN, born 1794 in Scotland, Presbyterian, a planter on Petersminde Estate, St Croix, Danish West Indies, 1841. [1841 Census]

MCCORQUODALE, ALEXANDER, a surgeon in Hanover, Jamaica, then in Larichban, Argyll, 1743. [NAS.CC2.10.142]

MCCORQUODALE, JOHN, in Lorn, St Elizabeth, Jamaica, testament confirmed with the Commissariat of Glasgow on 25 August 1772. [NAS]

MCCOURLIE, ..., in Jamaica, 1778. [NAS.CS16.1.174]

MCCOURTRIE, ALEXANDER, in St Thomas in the East, Jamaica, 1776. [NLS.Acc.8793]

MCCRACKEN, JOHN, a plasterer in Antigua, died 1800. [NAS.GD135/1693]

MCCROUGH, ..., planter of 1000 acres, St Andrew's parish, Jamaica, 1754. [NA.CO137/28]

MCCULLOCH, JOHN, marshal of Jamaica, ca.1750. [NAS.RH15.176.8]

MCCULLOCH, JOHN, eldest son of John McCulloch a farmer in Barnego, Stirlingshire, died at Rinidad Sagua La Grand, Cuba, 15 September 1868. [S#7873]

MCDERMEIT, ROBERT, Jamaica, was admitted as a burgess and guildsbrother of Ayr on 7 February 1784. [ABR]

MCDONALD, ALEXANDER, second son of Reverend H. F. McDonald in Strachan, Kincardineshire, died in Jamaica on 28 August 1874. [EC#28091]

MCDONALD, ALLAN, sixth son of John McDonald of Dalchosnie and his wife Mary Menzies, a planter in Jamaica, died 1825. [Clan Donald, p.437, Inverness, 1904]

MCDONALD, ANGUS, in Jamaica, 1850. [NAS.RD5.851.556]

MCDONALD, DONALD MACKAY, late planter in Jamaica, died in August 1791. [Clachn am Imbhir gravestone, Invermoriston, Inverness-shire]

MCDONALD, HUGH, in Jamaica 1765. [NAS.GD201.4.90]

MCDONALD, JOHN, a merchant in St Vincent, 1780. [NLS#8794]

MCDONALD, PATRICK, in Jamaica, son of Patrick McDonald a miller in Perth, testament confirmed with the Commissariat of Edinburgh on 9 September 1772. [NAS]

MCDONALD, WILLIAM, a surgeon in Trelawney, Jamaica, probate 3 January 1783 PCC

MCDONALD, WILLIAM, Lieutenant Governor of Fort Augusta, Jamaica, testament confirmed on 21

December 1791 with the Commissariat of Edinburgh.
[NAS]

MACDOUGAL, DUNCAN, a merchant in St Kitts, 1776-1778.
[NLS#8793/8794]

MCDOUGALL, ALLAN, a surgeon in St Kitts in December
1740. [CM#3262]

MCDOUGALL, ALLAN, son of Craiginich, died in Jamaica on
13 March 1786. [GM.IX.455.301]

MCDOUGALL, DOUGALL, in St Kitts, 1776. [NLS.Acc.8793]

MCDOUGALL, PATRICK, in St Kitts then in Gallaneech,
Argyll, 1780. [NAS.CS16.1.179]

MACDOUGALL, WILLIAM, St Kitts, graduated MD from
Edinburgh University in 1791. [EMG#23]

MCDOWAL, DANIEL, a merchant in St Vincent, 1799. [GA:T-
ARD#13/1]

MCDOWALL, ALEXANDER, in St Catherine's, Middlesex
County, Jamaica, 1818. [NAS.SC15.55.2]

MCDOWALL, JAMES, a planter in St Kitts, 1777. [NLS#8795]

MCDOWALL, JOHN, a merchant in St Vincent, 1780.
[NLS#8794]

MCDOWALL, Colonel WILLIAM, a planter in St Kitts, 1729-
1732. [NLS#8800]

MACDOWELL, LAURENCE, in Grenada, 1800.
[NAS.GD237.12.31]

MCDUFFIE, DUGALD, a merchant in Jamaica, married Janet
Campbell from Argyll, in Old Cambus, Berwickshire, on
13 April 1765. [Haddington Episcopal Register][Argyll
Sheriff Court Book #XVI, 20.3.1765]

MCEACHRAN, ARCHIBALD, a planter in Bladon County,
North Carolina, a Loyalist in 1776, settled in Jamaica by
1783. [NA.AO12.35.70]

MCEWAN, GEORGE, for 38 years a medical practitioner in
Grenada, died at 3 Frederick Street, Edinburgh, on 16
October 1834. [AJ#4529][Port of Menteith gravestone]

MCEWAN, ROBERT, from Glasgow, died in Port of Spain,
Trinidad, on 28 November 1843. [GSP#839]

MCFADYEAN, JAMES, a draper in Roseau, Dominica,
testament confirmed during 1868 in Edinburgh.
[NAS.SC70.1.139/740]

MCFADYEN, JAMES, born 3 May 1799 in Glasgow, son of
John McFadyen a merchant, educated at Glasgow
University in 1813, a lecturer from 1822 to 1824, a

physician and botanist in Jamaica, died there on 24 November 1850. [MAGU#271][Caribbeana#4/80]

MCFARLANE, ALEXANDER, a merchant in Jamaica, was admitted as a burgess and guildsbrother of Ayr on 4 April 1751. [ABR]

MACFARLANE, ANDREW, Black Morass, Jamaica, 1774. [NAS.NRAS#934/433]

MACFARLANE, DAVID, a planter in St Croix, 1776-1781, [NLS#8793/31]

MACFARLANE, DUNCAN, a planter in Jamaica, 1776-1778. [NLS#8793-4]

MACFARLANE, GEORGE, St Croix, graduated MD from Edinburgh University in 1803.[EMG#35]

MACFARLANE, HARRIET, daughter of Major James MacFarlane, and wife of William McKenzie at Morant Bay, Jamaica, testament confirmed with the Commissariat of Edinburgh on 22 December 1785. [NAS]

MCFARLANE, JAMES, in Jamaica, 1780. [NAS.CS16.1.179]

MACFARLANE, JAMES, Mayor of Castries, Member of HM Legislative Council, married Anna Maria Flora MacFarlane, second daughter of James MacFarlane senior, in Soufriese, St Lucia, on 14 February 1860. [S#1481]

MCFARLANE, JOHN, in Savannah la Mar, Jamaica, 1801. [NAS.AC7.75]

MCFARLANE, JOHN, LRCE Edinburgh, born 1821, died at Montego Bay, Jamaica, on 5 May 1862. [Dean gravestone, Edinburgh]

MACFARLANE, WALTER, a merchant in St Croix, 1776-1778. [NLS#8793/8794]

MCFARLANE, WALTER, died in Antigua on 26 September 1839. [SG#8/826]

MCFARQUHAR, Dr GEORGE, born 1741, a physician in Jamaica for 22 years, died 25 December 1786. [St James gravestone, Jamaica]

MCFEE, WILLIAM, born in 1832, son of William McFee [1788- 1869], died in Mandeville, Jamaica, on 2 January 1870. [Mochrum gravestone, Wigtownshire]

MACGILL, ROBERT, a merchant on Nevis, 1770-1780. [NLS#8793-4]

MCGILLVRAY, CHARLES CALDER, son of Reverend D. McGillvray, from Kilmalie, Inverness-shire, died in Grenada on 6 April 1845. [W#6/569]

MCGILLVRAY, JOHN, late in West Florida, then in Jamaica, 1787. [NAS.CS17.1.16/164]

MCGILIVRAY, WILLIAM, Hillside Estate, Vere, Jamaica, 1816. [NAS.NRAS#392/29/1]

MACGLASHAN, CHARLES, Jamaica, graduated MD from Edinburgh University in 1813. [EMG#47]

MCGOWAN, GEORGE, born 7 June 1774 in Garlieston, Wigton, father of Margaret, Isabella, Elizabeth and Caroline, died in Jamaica during June 1824. [Caribbeana#5/39]

MCGOWAN, WILLIAM, jr., a merchant in Jamaica then in Glasgow, testament confirmed with the Commissariat of Glasgow on 21 February 1770. [NAS]

MCGOWN, ALEXANDER, settled in Georgia 1766, a merchant, a Loyalist in 1776, settled at Montego Bay, Jamaica, by 1783. [NA.AO13.91.230]

MCGOWN, ALEXANDER, a merchant, son of baillie Alexander McGown in Rothesay, died in Kingston, Jamaica, on 2 June 1795. [GM.65.791]

MCGREGOR OF MCGREGOR, Sir JOHN ATHOLL, President of the Virgin Islands, died in Tortula on 11 May 1851. [EEC#22134]

MCGREGOR, NEIL, in Jamaica, testament confirmed with the Commissariat of Edinburgh on 19 September 1798. [NAS]

MACGREGOR, WILLIAM GORDON, born in Grantown on Spey 3 April 1801, a planter in St Vincent, died in Edinburgh on 15 September 1849. [Dean gravestone, Edinburgh]

MCILHOSE, JAMES, late a writer in Glasgow, then in Jamaica, 1796. [NAS.CS17.1.15/215]

MCINDOE, CHARLES, husband of Janet Buchanan, in St Vincent, then in Glasgow, 1853. [NAS.RS.Glasgow#3974]

MCINDOE, JOHN S., of Greenfield, St Thomas in the East, Jamaica, died at 10 Kirk Street, Glasgow, on 28 November 1838. [SG#7/720]

MCINTOSH, CHARLES, son of Alexander McIntosh of Blirvie, married Susanna Lawrence in St James, Jamaica, on 25 November 1757, father of Susanna, Elizabeth,

Susanna, John, George, Mary and Dehany.
[Caribeanna#3.160]

MACKINTOSH, DONALD, late in Jamaica, now in Greenock, 1841. [NAS.RS.Argyll#128]

MCINTOSH, DONALD, born 1779, late in Jamaica, died in Dunbarton on 28 July 1845. [SG#14/1424]

MCINTOSH, DUNCAN, settled in Dominica in 1761, land grant in St Ann's parish in 1765, moved to St Pierre, Martinique, July 1774.
[NAS.NRAS#771/306][NAS.GD126, box 4]

MCINTOSH, JAMES, a merchant in Jamaica then in Inverness-shire, 1780. [NAS.CS16.1.179]

MACKINTOSH, JOHN, in St Thomas in the East, Jamaica, 1776. [NLS.Acc.8793]

MCINTOSH, MARY ELLIS, daughter of James Macintosh, master builder with the Trinidad Public Works Department, died in Port of Spain on 28 February 1873. [EC#27614]

MCINTOSH, WILLIAM, of Geddes, late in Jamaica, granted the lands of Easter Geddes on 3 February 1800. [NAS.RGS.131.70]

MCINTYRE, ARCHIBALD, born 16 August 1774 in Glen Orchy, Argyll, son of Reverend Joseph McIntyre and Christian McVean, settled in Jamaica. [F.4.87]

MCINTYRE, ARCHIBALD, died on Kendal Estate, Hanover, Jamaica, on 18 December 1809. [PC#69]

MCINTYRE, DANIEL, clerk or book-keeper to the firm of McNeil, Saddler and Claxton in St Kitts, 1760. [NAS.CS96/4370/30]

MCINTYRE, DANIEL or DONALD, born 8 November 1778 in Glen Orchy, Argyll, son of Reverend Joseph McIntyre and Christian McVean, died in Jamaica during July 1797. [F.4.87]

MCINTYRE, JOHN, eldest son of Donald McIntyre a craftsman at Antigua Bay, Jamaica, matriculated at Glasgow University in 1805. [MAGU#212]

MCINTYRE, PATRICK, born 14 February 1773 in Glen Orchy, Argyll, son of Reverend Joseph McIntyre and Christian McVean, settled in Jamaica. [F.4.87]

MACKAY, CHARLES, third son of James T. Mackay a hat manufacturer in Edinburgh, died on Plantain Garden River Estate, Jamaica, on 27 May 1873. [EC#27686]

MACKAY, DANIEL, born 1757, late of St Croix, died in
   Glebeside Row, Glasgow, on 15 May 1839. [SG#8/768]
MACKAY, DONALD, in Antigua, 1804. [NAS.GD87/2/27]
MCKAY, DONALD, factor, Rosenberg Villa, Tain, St Vincent,
   1855. [NAS.242/70/6/187]
MACKAY, GEORGE, planter of 11 acres, St Andrew's parish,
   Jamaica, 1754. [NA.CO137/28]
MACKAY, JAMES, a physician and surgeon in St Thomas in
   the East, Jamaica, testament confirmed with the
   Commissariat of Edinburgh on 13 August 1799. [NAS]
MACKAY, JOHN, a planter in Tobago, 1778-1779.
   [NLS#8794]
MACKAY, WILLIAM PATRICK, son of James T. Mackay, 21
   Danube Street, Edinburgh, died on Wheelerfield Estate,
   Jamaica, on 1 August 1860. [S#1621]
MACKEAND, ALEXANDER, attorney in Kingston, Jamaica,
   son of George MacKeand, late of Jamaica, and nephew
   of late Robert MacKeand of Jamaica, sons of deceased
   John MacKeand baillie of Wigtown, 5 July 1773.
   [NAS.B72.1.2]
MCKECHNIE, JOHN, a millwright from Greenock, then in
   Westmoreland County, Jamaica, died before 1800.
   [GA.T-ARD#13/1]
MACKECHNIE, SOMERSALL, second son of Claud
   MacKechnie a merchant in St Kitts, matriculated at
   Glasgow University in 1802. [MAGU#207]
MACKECHNIE, WILLIAM, eldest son of Claud MacKechnie a
   merchant in St Kitts, matriculated at Glasgow University
   in 1804. [MAGU#211]
MACKELL, ROBERT, a merchant in Tobago, 1780.
   [NLS#8794]
MCKELLAR, DUNCAN, in Hampden, Tobago, died by 1807.
   [GA.T-ARD#13/1]
MCKELLAR, DUNCAN, a planter on Hermitage Estate,
   Tobago, 1836. [NA.T71/1572]
MCKENNA, WILLIAM, a planter on Belle Gardens Estate,
   Tobago, 1836. [NA.T47/1572]
MCKENZIE, ALEXANDER, a Jacobite rebel, transported from
   London to Antigua on the Prince George, master James
   Nairn, on 14 January 1748, landed 16 March 1748.
   [NA.T53/44]

MCKENZIE, COLIN, of Strathcathro, former merchant in Jamaica, 1764, son of Kenneth McKenzie of Dalmore. [NAS.RS35.xx.335][NAS.NRAS#0771/762]

MCKENZIE, D., in Kingston, Jamaica, 1809, brother in law of Alexander Dingwall in Caninish. [NAS.NRAS#2177/6179]

MCKENZIE, DANIEL, a Jacobite rebel, transported from Liverpool to Jamaica on the Elizabeth, master Daniel Cole, on 7 February 1748, landed 21 March 1748. [NA.T53/44]

MCKENZIE, DUNCAN, in St Vincent, married Elspet, only daughter of James Paul a ship-owner in Banff, there on 25 April 1837. [AJ#4660]

MCKENZIE, FARQUHAR, a planter in Jamaica, 1715. [NAS.RD4.117.589]

MCKENZIE, GEORGE, late a planter in Jamaica, then in America, 1803, eldest son of Colin McKenzie a writer in Dingwall. [NAS.CS17.1.22/370]; 1787, [NAS,RS.Ross#195]

MCKENZIE, HECTOR, a Jacobite rebel, transported from London to Antigua on the Prince George, master James Nairn, on 14 January 1748, landed 16 March 1748. [NA.T53/44]

MCKENZIE, Dr JOHN, brother of Colin McKenzie of Stracathro, Angus, late planter in Jamaica, 1764. [NAS.NRAS#771/191]

MCKENZIE, JOHN, an attorney, son of Alexander McKenzie of Inchcoulter, died in Kingston, Jamaica, in December 1780. [GM#IV/86]

MCKENZIE, JOHN, in Jamaica, nephew of Lieutenant Daniel Mack, testament confirmed with the Commissariat of Edinburgh on 9 February 1785. [NAS]

MACKENZIE, Mrs MARGARET, daughter of Lord Oliphant, died on 6 April 1800 in Spanish Town, Jamaica, [GM#70.797]

MCKENZIE, MARGARET, wife of Hugh Campbell a teacher, eldest daughter of Hector McKenzie a teacher in Anderston, died on Troumassie Estate, St Lucia, on 25 April 1839. [SG#8/786]

MACKENZIE, RODERICK, son of Kenneth MacKenzie of Redcastle, died in Jamaica 1801. [GM#71.483]

MACKENZIE, THOMAS, Jamaica, graduated MD from Edinburgh University in 1814. [EMG#48]

MCKENZIE, WILLIAM, Grenada, graduated MD from
Edinburgh University in 1809. [EMG#42]

MACKIE, GEORGE, died in St Vincent on 1 August 1846.
[AJ#5151]

MACKIE, WILLIAM, in Jamaica, deed 15 January 1819.
[NAS.CC16.9.12, 77]

MACKIE, WILLIAM, a merchant in Grenada, 1808. [GA.T-
ARD#13/1]

MCKINDLAY, Dr ALEXANDER, in Jamaica then in Leith,
testament confirmed in October 1774 with the
Commissariat of Edinburgh. [NAS][NAS.CS96/1834, 57]

MCKINLAY, FINLAY, from Greenock to Antigua on the
Joanna, master James Brown, 9 September 1790.
[NAS.E504.15.56]

MCKINLAY, ROBERT, merchant in Antigua, co-owner of the
Mercury of Greenock 1792. [NAS.CE60.11.3/59]

MCKINLAY, WILLIAM, St Kitts, graduated MA in Aberdeen
on 31 March 1772. [AUL]

MCKINNA, JOHN, a merchant in Edinburgh, then in Jamaica,
testament confirmed on 31 January 1766 with the
Commissariat of Edinburgh. [NAS]

MCKINNON, CHARLES WILLIAM, in Antigua 1757.
[DA.Ogilvie pp/24]

MCKITTRICK, JAMES, in Antigua, 1753. [NAS.CS96/645]

MCKNIGHT, THOMAS, merchant in Tobago, co-owner of the
High Flyer of Greenock, 1799. [NAS.CE60.11.6/32]

MCKOWEN, ARCHIBALD, Jamaica, graduated MD from
Edinburgh University in 1818. [EMG#56]

MCLACHLAN, DUGALD, sometime in Jamaica, then in
Callart, Argyll, testament confirmed in 1800 with the
Commissariat of Argyll. [NAS.CC2.3.12]

MCLACHLAN, ..., an overseer at Hampden, Jamaica, in
1782. [NLS.MS10925/5]

MCLAGAN, ALEXANDER, died in Jamaica before February
1792. [GCr#70]

MACLAINE, JOHN, in Kingston, Jamaica, 1788.
[NAS.GD174/1418]

MACLAINE, LAUCHLAN, to Jamaica in 1789.
[NAS.GD174/1431]

MCLAREN, ALEXANDER, in St Kitts, testament confirmed
1868 Edinburgh. [NAS.SC70.1.140/13]

MCLAREN, ANN, daughter of John McLaren a planter in
Jamaica, married James MacLennan a watchmaker in

Edinburgh, there on 22 December 1776. [Edinburgh Marriage Register]

MCLAREN, JOHN, died in Jamaica 1793. [Canongate gravestone]

MCLARTY, ALEXANDER, a physician in Kingston, Jamaica, will refers to his reputed daughter Eliza MacLarty in Campbeltown, Argyll, his sister Margaret, his sons Alexander, Colin, his daughter Isabella, his brother Colin MacLarty in Campbeltown, his executors brother Colin, friends John and Richard Dick in Edinburgh, Dugald Campbell in St Andrews parish, Reverend Alexander Campbell in St Andrews parish, and Lewis Johnston, a physician and surgeon in Kingston, subscribed 13 December 1820. [NAS.SC53.56.3]

MACLARTY, ALEXANDER, MD, in Kingston, Jamaica, will, 25 May 1821. [NAS.SC53/56/3.18]

MACLARTY, ELIZA, daughter of Alexander MacLarty MD in Jamaica, 1822. [NAS.RS10.PR42/32]

MCLAUCHLAN, DANIEL, a minister in Ardnamurchan, Argyll, 1734 to 1737, died in Jamaica on 16 May 1745. [F.4.1060]

MCLAUGHLAN, DUGALD, in Jamaica then in Callait, Inverness, testament confirmed on 4 July 1800 with the Commissariat of Argyll. [NAS]

MCLAUGHLAN, Captain HUGH, from Glasgow, died in Jamaica, 1755. [GJ#752]

MCLAVERTY, Reverend COLIN, married Mary Elizabeth East, daughter of Hinton East, in Jamaica on 1 January 1846. [PC#2008]; '25 years the incumbent of St Peter's, Jamaica', died at Clifton Passage, Jamaica, on 15 August 1869. [S#8160]

MCLAVERTY, ..., son of Mr McLaverty from Keill, Argyll, was born in Chestervale, Jamaica, on 27 July 1855. [EEC#322788]

MCLEA, FINLAY, in Antigua, 1760. [DA.Ogilvie pp33]

MCLEAN, ALLAN, born in 1824, youngest son of John McLean a merchant in Greenock, died in Trinidad during 1838. [SG#8/741]

MCLEAN, ARCHIBALD, Lieutenant Colonel of the 7th West Indian Regiment, 1814. [NAS.SC51.50.2.1.128]

MCLEAN, HUGH, a merchant in Jamaica, 1788. [NAS.CS17.1.7/133]

MCLEAN, HUGH, in Spanish Town, Jamaica, dead by 1844. [NAS.RS38.GR2255/120]

MCLEAN, JOHN, a merchant in Jamaica, was admitted as a burgess and guildsbrother of Ayr on 4 April 1751. [ABR]

MCLEAN, JOHN, born 1776, died in Carriacou 18 February 1816. [Alness gravestone]

MCLEAN, ..., son of Reverend Daniel McLean, was born at Hampden Manse, Jamaica, on 19 December 1861. [S#2052]

MCLEAN, ..., was born at Hampden Manse, Jamaica, on 11 April 1863. [S#2468]

MACLEAN & MOORE, merchants in Jamaica, 1778-1780. [NLS#8793/4]

MCLELLAN, JANET, widow of William Lauder a teacher of humanity in Barbados, and daughter of Robert McLellan of Summerhall, 1779. [NAS.C\S16.1.175]

MCLEOD, ALEXANDER, born 1789, died in Waterloo House, St Vincent, in February 1861. [St Vincent Death Register #11]

MCLEOD, GEORGE, son of John McLeod, late of Milne, Cruden and Company in Aberdeen, chief clerk at the government office in Castries, died in St Lucia on 14 February 1864. [AJ:23.3.1864]

MCLEOD, HUGH, a merchant in Aux cayes, St Domingo, and in Kingston, Jamaica, died in 1818. [NAS.CS235/ui.8]

MCLEOD, JAMES, son of Hugh McLeod of Geanies, a planter in St Vincent around 1776. [NLS#19297]

MCLEOD, JOHN, in Colbecks, St Dorothy, Jamaica, married Margaret McLeod, daughter of Roderick McLeod, in Edinburgh on 28 November 1773. [Edinburgh Marriage Register]

MCLEOD, JOHN, in Tobago, husband of Janet Alexander Stewart, 1817. [NAS.SC53.56.1]

MCLEOD, WILLIAM WATSON, born 1819, nephew of Henry McLeod, Provost Marshal General, and eldest son of John McLeod, Gordon's Mills, Aberdeen, died in St Lucia, on 24 August 1840. [AJ#4849]

MCLERAN, Dr ALEXANDER, was drowned crossing the Montego River, Jamaica, before February 1792. [GCr#70]

MCMIKIN, ROBERT, in Kingston, Jamaica, 1767. [NAS.GD180.634]

MCMILLAN, ALEXANDER, eldest son of late Hugh McMillan a clothier in Glasgow, died in Kingston, Jamaica, 16 September 1842. [SG.XI.1080][GSP#779]

MCMURCHY, JOHN, a merchant in Jamaica, moved to London by 1766. [Charleston, SC, Misc. Records. 1766/370]

MCNAB, ALEXANDER, in Jamaica around 1800, brother of Duncan McNab in Greenock. [NAS.NRAS#0888/103/2]

MCNAB, CHARLES, from Jamaica, married Janet Buchanan, daughter of Douglas Buchanan of Craigievorn, Stirlingshire, in Edinburgh on 1 October 1792. [Edinburgh Marriage Register]

MCNAB, Dr GILBERT, third son of William McNab of the Royal Botanical Gardens in Edinburgh, died in St Ann's, Jamaica, on 21 January 1860. [S#1434]

MCNAB, JAMES, late in Jamaica, married Margaret, daughter of Malcolm McNeil of Ardelister, in Islay on 27 February 1804. [CM#13029]

MCNEIL, HECTOR, in Antigua, 1753. [NAS.CS96/645]

MCNEIL, NEIL, in Hanover, Jamaica, 1749, father of John McNeil. [NAS.PS3.11.161]; testament confirmed on 8 May 1749 with the Commissariat of Glasgow. [NAS]

MCNEILL, JAMES, in Tobago, 1800. [NAS.CS18.715.15]

MCNEILL, JOHN, natural son of Neil McNeill, sometime in the parish of Hanover, Jamaica, died in 1749. [NAS.PS3.11/161]

MCNEILL, LACHLAN, son of Hector and Margaret McNeill in Saltpans, Machrahanish, Argyll, a merchant who died in Jamaica 1798. [SG.32.2.56]

MCNEILL, NEILL, sometime a merchant in Bristol then in St Kitts, brother of Malcolm McNeill of Ardlally, Islay, 1768, 1774. [NAS.CS27/907, 6][NAS.CC12.2.2]

MCNEILL, NEIL, of Ardylamie, a merchant planter in Jamaica, later in Glasgow, testament confirmed with the Commissariat of Glasgow on 16 December 1785. [NAS]

MCNEILL, SADDLER AND CLAXTON, merchants in St Kitts, 1758-1781. [NAS.CS96.4370; CS237.T4/1]

MCNERNEY, MATTHEW, born in 1787, a land surveyor in Clarendon, Jamaica, died on 14 January 1814. [Wigtown gravestone]

MCNICOL, DUGALD, Captain of the Royal Regiment of Foot in St Lucia, 1832. [NAS.SC51.50.2.3.139]

MCNISH, JAMES, died in Castries, St Lucia, on 1 July 1839. [SG#8/795]

MCPHADZEAN, ANGUS, a planter in Westmoreland parish, Jamaica, son and executor of Catherine McKewan spouse of Donald McPhadzean in Cuilichnuick, Argyll, edict of executry, 1785. [NAS.CC2.8.88, 6]

MCPHERSON, ANGUS, a prisoner in Edinburgh Tolbooth indented with John Ramsay a merchant in Glasgow for service in Jamaica, 10 September 1726. [NAS,HH11.15]

MACPHERSON, CAROLINA EVINA, eldest daughter of John MacPherson-McNiel of Kingston, Jamaica, married James Hay Campbell, Major of the Highland Light Infantry, in Kilburn on 17 October 1867. [S#7558]

MCPHERSON, DONALD, Unity Valley, Jamaica, 1774. [NAS.NRAS#771/166]

MCPHERSON, EVAN, from Kingussie, 'emigrated 30 years ago', died in Clarendon, Jamaica, on 3 January 1840. [AJ#4813]

MCPHERSON, JOHN, from Dalwhinnie then in Jamaica, 1779. [NAS.CS16.1.175]

MCQUEEN, DANIEL, planter of 800 acres, St Andrew's parish, Jamaica, 1754. [NA.CO137/28]

MCQUHAE, RICHARD, born 21 December 1766 in St Quivox, son of Reverend William McQuhae and his wife Elizabeth Park, died in Jamaica on 9 March 1805. [F.3.66]

MCRAE, ALEXANDER, born 1735, died in Jamaica on 3 March 1796. [Canongate gravestone]

MCTAIR, WILLIAM, in St Kitts, 1776. [NLS.Acc8793/28]

MCTAVISH, JOHN G., in Tobago 1849. [NAS.GD1.380.1.52]

MCVICAR, ALEXANDER, from Argyll, died in Port Royal, Jamaica, before 1806. [GA#AGN.321]

MCVICAR, ARCHIBALD, born 1819, son of Neil McVicar of Ardishaig, died in Trinidad April 1840. [Lochgilphead gravestone]

MCVICAR, or AFFLECK, JAMES, in St Thomas in the East, Jamaica, eldest son of late Robert McVicar, an excise officer in Stranraer, and his wife Mary, only child of James Affleck of Edingham, 1773. [NAS.CS16.1.154/77]

MCVICAR, JOHN, from Argyll, emigrated via Bristol to Jamaica in 1793, settled on Good Hope Estate, Trelawney, Jamaica. [SRA#AGN.321]

MCVICAR, Dr RONALD, a physician late of Dominica, died in Edinburgh on 17 April 1797. [CM#11801]

MCWALTER, DUNCAN, a merchant in Jamaica, deceased by 1771. [Argyll Sheriff Court Book #XVII, 13.6.1771]

MCWILLIAM, ANNA ELIZA, daughter of Alexander McWilliam late of Jamaica sometime of Grenada, died in Elgin on 26 February 1840. [AJ#4809]

MCWILLIAM, JOHN, born 1821, son of William McWilliam, a farmer in Ring, Wigtownshire, died in Nassau on 14 July 1864; his wife Agnes born in 1821, died on the Isle of Whithorn on 12 June 1899. [Whithorn gravestone, Wigtownshire]

MACK, THOMAS, in Kingston, Jamaica, from 1786 to 1795, later farmer in Gordon Mains, Berwickshire. [NAS.CS29/912]

MAIR, JAMES, West Indies, graduated MD from Edinburgh University in 1795. [EMG#26]

MAITLAND, GEORGE, a merchant in St Vincent, 1799. [GA:T-ARD#13/1]

MALCOLM, DUGALD, at Pell River, Jamaica, 1774, [Argyll Sheriff Court Book #XVII, 13.5.1774]; of Poltiver, Jamaica, 1778. [NAS.CS16.1.173/50]

MALCOLM, HUGH, deceased, late a merchant in Jamaica, son of John Malcolm and Catherine Campbell, 25 June 1773. [Argyll Sheriff Court Book #XVII,13.5.1774]

MALCOLM, HUGH, in Jamaica, then in Glasgow, testament confirmed on 10 February 1795 with the Commissariat of Glasgow. [NAS.CC9.7.75]

MALCOLM, NEIL, a merchant in Jamaica, 1774, [Argyll Sheriff Court Book #XVII, 13.5.1774]

MALCOLM, ..., daughter of Andrew Malcolm was born in Grenada on 8 September 1842. [SG#11/1132]

MANEY, PETER, in Grenada 1811. [NAS.SC48.49.25.3/110,114]

MANN, JOHN, a planter on Bellisle, Westmoreland, Jamaica, 1830. [NAS.SC48.49.25.28/110]

MANSON, DAVID, son of John Manson and Elizabeth Keay, died in Jamaica on 2 July 1821. [Perth, Greyfriars, gravestone]

MARQUIS, ALEXANDER, born 1759, a carpenter, died 22 July 1799. [Palisades gravestone, Port Royal, Jamaica]

MARSHALL, ANDREW, a gardener, emigrated via Greenock to St Vincent's on the Nancy, Captain Buchanan, in January 1778

MARSHALL, JOHN, late of Jamaica, then in Angus by 1777. [NAS.RS35.xxvi,181]

MARSHALL, THOMAS, born in Glasgow son of Robert Marshall a merchant, educated at Glasgow University in 1791, manager of the Frome Estate, Jamaica, died 15 July 1802. [Caribbeana#4.17][MAGU#165]

MARTIN, GEORGE, in Tortula, and his executor there John Hanley, 1821. [NAS.CS17.1.40/8]

MARTIN, JAMES, born in Aberdeenshire, 'for many years a planter in Grenada', died on board the Ferrier on passage to Tobago in 1838. [AJ:13.2.1839]

MARTIN, ROBERT, in Antigua 1757. [DA.Ogilvie pp/14]

MATHER, JOHN, a merchant in Kingston, Jamaica, 1779, [NAS.CS16.1.174]; then in Hamilton 1780, [NAS.CS16.1.177]; 2 October 1816. [NAS.SC37.59.3/192]

MATTHEW, SAMUEL, born 1837, eldest son of James Matthew of the High Court of Justiciary in Edinburgh, died in Port of Spain, Trinidad, on 30 November 1859. [CM#21615]

MATTHEWS, MATTHEW, a Jacobite rebel, transported from Liverpool to Jamaica on 7 February 1748, landed 21 March 1748. [NA.T53/44]

MAXTON, PETER, killed by pirates in San Domingo, pre-1800. [NAS.CS22.780.26]

MAXWELL, JOHN, in Tobago, died 1794. [NAS.NRAS#3626/530][NAS.GD171/530]

MAXWELL, JOHN, late in Jamaica, son of William Maxwell, was admitted as a burgess of Dundee on 4 February 1818. [Dundee Burgess Roll]

MAXWELL, PATRICK, in Grenada, 1776. [NLS.Acc.8793]

MAXWELL, PETER, in Grenada, 1776. [NLS.Acc8793/5]

MAXWELL, WILLIAM, in Antigua 1753. [NAS.CS96/644]

MAXWELL, ..., a planter in Tobago, 1800. [GA:T-ARD#13/1]

MEIKLE, JOHN, a surgeon in Jamaica, son of John Meikle and Mary Meikle in Paisley, 1779. [NAS.CS16.1.179]

MEIKLE, JOHN, a surgeon-physician in St Dorothy's parish, Middlesex, Jamaica, June 1817, dead by 1822. [NAS.CS17.1.36/508; 42/18]

MEIN, JAMES, late in Jamaica, now in Newstead, Roxburghshire, 1820. [NAS.RS, Roxburgh#5629]

MELVILLE, ALEXANDER, St Vincent, graduated MD in Aberdeen on 26 December 1795. [AUL]

MELVILLE, JOHN, settled in Tobago, 1774. [NAS.NRAS#3626/16]

MELVILLE, JOHN, St Vincent, graduated MD from Edinburgh University in 1811. [EMG#44]

MELVILLE, ROBERT, late Governor General of Jamaica, 1772. [NAS.RS27.200.240]

MENZIES, ALEXANDER, planter of 81 acres, St Andrew's parish, Jamaica, 1754. [NA.CO137/28]

MENZIES, ARCHIBALD, in Kingston, Jamaica, granted the lands of Pitnacree on 2 June 1809; in Kingston, Jamaica, 1810. [NAS.RGS.140.16.24][NAS.SC48.49.25.2/196]

MENZIES, JEAN, daughter of William Menzies in Jamaica, married Alexander Fraser of Moremount, in Edinburgh on 11 March 1764. [Edinburgh Marriage Register]

MERCER, ALEXANDER, a merchant in Edinburgh then in Jamaica, testament confirmed on 16 May 1788 with the Commissariat of Edinburgh. [NAS]

MERCER, Lieutenant LAWRENCE, born in Gask, son of Reverend Lawrence Mercer and his wife Jean Lindsay, died in Jamaica during August 1742. [F.4.274]

MERCHANT, WILLIAM COPLAND, born 1821, son of Richard Merchant (1771-1822) and Elizabeth Wilson (died 1854), an engineer, died in Tobago on 5 September 1862. [St Nicholas gravestone, Aberdeen]

MIDDLETON, GEORGE, born in 1810, son of the late Reverend George Middleton in Midmar, Aberdeenshire, died in Jamaica on 28 September 1852. [AJ:24.11.1852]

MILLER, ARCHIBALD, a mason in the West Indies from 1769 to 1781. [NA.AO100/348]

MILLER, DAVID, surgeon in Westmorland, Jamaica, then in Bristol, 1753. [NAS.RS35.xvii.546]

MILLER, GEORGE, in Long Island, Bahamas, 1795. [NAS.CS17.1.14/99]

MILLER, JAMES, Jamaica, married Elizabeth Fordyce, daughter of Robert Fordyce a merchant in Aberdeen, in Edinburgh on 20 June 1781. [Edinburgh Marriage Register]

MILLER, JAMES, merchant in Greenock, to the West Indies, a partner in McAlister and Miller, Greenock and St Thomas, 1796. [NAS.CS58.61.22]

MILLER, JAMES, merchant in New Providence, co-owner of the Glasgow of Glasgow, 1799,the Hannah of Glasgow 1799, and the Diana of Glasgow, 1801. [NAS.CE60.11.6/83/87, 7/24]

MILLER, JOHN, a merchant in Glasgow then in Jamaica, 1800, [NAS.CS18.710.15]; late a merchant in Kingston, Jamaica, then in Glasgow, 1821. [NAS.CS17.1.40/269]

MILLER, JOHN, in Jamaica, later in Breadiesholm 1813. [NAS.RS.Argyll#2266]

MILLER, ROBERT, a planter in Portland, Jamaica, then in Tobago 1790. [NAS.CS16.1.173/405]

MILLER, ROBERT, in Jamaica, thereafter in Glasgow, testament 8 February 1821. [NAS.CC9.7.81.134]

MILLER, ROBERT A., born 1817, eldest son of James Miller in Cumbrae, died in Trinidad on 26 February 1844. [GSP#853]

MILLER, THOMAS, in Jamaica, 1785. [NAS.B41.7.8.325]

MILLER, Dr WILLIAM, Antigua, was admitted as a burgess and guildsbrother of Ayr on 17 October 1767. [ABR]

MILLER, WILLIAM, born 7 March 1767, son of Reverend Thomas Miller and his wife Beatrix Colquhoun, in Lerwick, Shetland Islands, died in Spanish Town, Jamaica, on 24 October 1791. [Glasgow Courier#57] [F#7.286]

MILLER, WILLIAM, born in 1801, son of Hugh Millar [1751-1824] and Jean ... [1760-1830], died in Grenada on 23 March 1833. [Kilmaurs gravestone, Ayrshire]

MILLER, Dr WILLIAM, in Antigua, dead by 1818. [NAS.RS54.GR1113/272]

MILLIKEN, WILLIAM, in St Kitts, 1757. [NAS.GD237/12/47]

MILROY, JOHN, born in 1784, son of John Milroy and Mary McCulloch, died in Dominica on 3 June 1804. [Whithorn Old gravestone, Wigtownshire]

MITCHELL, WILLIAM, born during 1763 at East Seaton, St Vigeans, Angus, settled in St Croix around 1784, died at Buss End, St Croix, on 16 March 1834. [AJ#4514]

MITCHELL, ALEXANDER, a merchant in Antigua 1778. [NAS.CS16.1.173/159]

SCOTS IN THE WEST INDIES, 1707-1857, VOLUME II

MITCHELL, JAMES, youngest son of John Mitchell in Pitt
Street, Edinburgh, died in Spanish Town, Jamaica, in
1816. [S#10]

MITCHELL, ROBERT, a planter in Tobago, 1800. [GA:T-
ARD#13/1]

MITCHELL, WALTER, a Jacobite rebel, transported from
London to Antigua on the Prince George, master James
Nairn, on 14 January 1748, landed 16 March 1748.
[NA.T53/44]

MITCHELL, WILLIAM, in Bushy Park, Jamaica, admitted as a
burgess of Edinburgh, on 23 July 1794. [Edinburgh
Burgess Roll]

MITCHELL, ..., daughter of G. A. Mitchell, born in Carriacou
on 2 May 1851. [AJ#5397]

MITCHELL, ..., daughter of Rev. George Mitchell, was born
in St George, Grenada, 4 June 1868. [S#7776]

MOFFAT, ALEXANDER, prisoner in Edinburgh Tolbooth,
indented with John Ramsay a merchant in Glasgow for
service in Jamaica, September 1726. [NAS.HH11.15]

MOFFAT, ..., daughter of John S. Moffat, was born in
Soufriere, St Lucia, on 8 May 1849. [SG#18/1828]

MOIR, ALEXANDER, in Jamaica, 1845. [NAS.GD171.1301]

MOIR, GEORGE, merchant in Jamaica, co-owner of the
Magnet of Glasgow, 1800. [NAS.CE60.11.6/18]

MOIR, HENRY, a Jacobite rebel, transported from London to
Antigua on the Prince George, master James Nairn, on
14 January 1748, landed 16 March 1748. [NA.T53/44]

MOIR, ROBERT, a Jacobite rebel, transported from London to
Antigua on the Prince George, master James Nairn, on
14 January 1748, landed 16 March 1748. [NA.T53/44]

MONCREIFF, DAVID, born 13 January 1691 in Kirkwall,
Orkney, son of Harry Moncrieff, a merchant, and his wife
Barbara Erberie, settled in St Catherine's, Jamaica,
1730, Provost Marshal of Jamaica, died before February
1739 in Jamaica. [NAS.GD237.2.21/2] [Moncrieff and
the Moncrieffes, p271, {Edinburgh, 1929}]

MONTEATH, ANDREW, a carpenter, died in Falmouth,
Jamaica, on 11 June 1797. [GM#67.800]

MONTEITH, ARCHIBALD DOUGLAS, son of Walter Monteith
of Kipp, Stirlingshire, emigrated to St Vincent in 1775.
[NAS.RD4.218.870]

MONTEITH, WILLIAM, born 1807, died in Kingston, Jamaica,
on 26 April 1841. [GSP#668]

MONTGOMERIE, ROBERT, born 1785, eldest son of Hugh Montgomerie of Braidley and his wife Elizabeth Barclay, in Dalry, Ayrshire, died in Jamaica. [HAF

MONTGOMERY, CHARLES, Rozelle Estate, St Thomas, Jamaica, 1764. [NAS.NRAS#3572/2/18]

MONTGOMERY, Colonel CHARLES, in Jamaica, died during February 1804, testament confirmed on 9 October 1805 with the Commissariat of Edinburgh. [NAS.CC8.8.136]

MONTGOMERY, ROBERT, a merchant in St Croix, 1809, 1822. [NAS.CS239/S49/9; CS17.1.41/643]

MONTGOMERY, WILLIAM, in Antigua 1753. [NAS.CS96/644]

MOODIE, JEAN, daughter of James Moodie in Jamaica, married William Keith, son of Dr William Keith in South Carolina, in Edinburgh on 12 March 1769. [Edinburgh Marriage Register]

MOORE, WILLIAM, applied to settle in Havana, Cuba, on 9 June 1856. [NAC.Cartas de Domocilio]

MORGAN, JAMES, of Bonnymuir, born 1756, son of George Morgan (1722-1783) and Elspit Morgan (1714-1792), '25 years in Jamaica', died 15 July 1823. [St Nicholas gravestone, Aberdeen]

MORGAN, WILLIAM, merchant in Jamaica, co-owner of the Favourite of Greenock, 1700. [NAS.CE60.11.6/22]

MORRICE, ROBERT, son of Reverend William Morrice and his wife Helen Paterson in Kincardine O'Neil, educated at Marischal College, Aberdeen, from 1779-1783, later a planter in Jamaica. [MCA.II.355]

MORRIS, ALEXANDER, a planter in Cornwall County, Jamaica, who died before 1796. [NAS.CS16.1.201/440]

MORRIS, HENRY, a vintner in Tobago, 1800. [GA:T-ARD#13/1]

MORRIS, LOUDEN, eldest son of Andrew Morris a surgeon in Glasgow, educated at Glasgow University in 1768, later a surgeon on Green Island, Jamaica, 1788. [MAGU#87]

MORRIS, MARY MELBOROUGH, wife of George Horne from Edinburgh, died in Basseterre, St Kitts, on 12 May 1869. [S#8060]

MORRIS, WILLIAM, a planter in Tobago, 1800. [GA:T-ARD#13/1]

MORRISON, AGNES, born during 1823, daughter of John Morrison, the Assistant Clerk of Session, wife of Donald Mackenzie Morrison a merchant in Antigua, died in St John's, Antigua, on 18 May 1853. [EEC#22447]

MORRISON, ALEXANDER, a planter in Cornwall County, Jamaica, 1793. [NAS.CS17.1.12/253]

MORRISON, ALEXANDER, born in 1826, from Turriff, Aberdeenshire, died in Kingston, St Vincent, on 1 November 1863. [AJ:9.12.1863]

MORRISON, ARCHIBALD, a merchant in Jamaica, dead by 1804. [NAS.AC7.77]

MORRISON, DONALD MCK., married Agnes, daughter of John Morrison, Register House, Edinburgh, at St John's, Antigua, on 8 April 1851. [EEC#22118]

MORRISON, GEORGE, late in Jamaica, then in Aberdeen, 1796. [NAS.GD105.51]

MORRISON, GEORGE, late of Tobago, 1814, son of Alexander Morrison of Bogrie who died in September 1801. [NAS.NRAS#3585/4/2/32]

MORRISON, JAMES, a merchant in Tobago, 1801. [NAS.RS8.GR628/52][NAS.NRAS#3585/7/11/2]

MORRISON, JAMES, MD, born in Inverurie, Aberdeenshire, late of the East India Company, then a farmer in the Vale of Alford, Aberdeenshire, emigrated to Grenada in 1858, died at the Carenage, Grenada, on 2 January 1860. [AJ:8.2.1860]

MORRISON, JESSIE, second daughter of William Morrison, Queen's Terrace, Ayr, married James Drennan from Springfield, in San Fernando, Trinidad, on 5 June 1878. [EC#29254]

MORRISON, JOHN, in Antigua, 1753. [NAS.CS96/644]

MORRISON, ROBERT, born in 1792, a farmer, applied to settle in Havana, Cuba, on 7 November 1818. [NAC.Cartas de Domocilio]

MORRISON, WILLIAM, eldest son of John Morrison factor at Craigievar, a baker in Aberdeen later in Port Morant, Jamaica, 1799. [NAS.CS26.909.29]

MORRISON, WILLIAM, a saddler from Glasgow, died in Grenada on 18 June 1831. [GkAd#3683]

MORTON, ALICE BISHOP, born 1843, wife of Charles Goldie HM Customs late of Greenock, died in Kingston, Jamaica, 16 November 1869. [S#8232]

MOSMAN, ..., a merchant in Bermuda, 1814, son of Hugh Mosman of Auchtyfardle. [NAS.NRAS#2177/1623]

MOWAT, CHARLES EGGLESTONE, son of the late James Mowat a merchant in Aberdeen, died in Tobago on 27 February 1836. [AJ: 27.4.1836]

MUDIE, ALEXANDER, born 1763, late of Jamaica, died at 35 Albany Street, Edinburgh, 17 February 1844.
[Edinburgh, New Calton gravestone]

MUIR, EBENEZER, fourth son of Dr George Muir minister in Paisley, in Savannah la Mar, Jamaica, 1784.
[NAS.SC58.61.15]

MUIR, FREELAND, son of Andrew Muir a merchant in Kirkcudbright, died in St Vincent, 1797. [EWJ#1]

MUIR, Dr JOHN, in Antigua 1757. [DA.Ogilvie pp/24]

MUIR, JOHN, from Antigua, graduated MD at Glasgow University in 1790, [RGG#457]; was admitted as a burgess and guilds-brother of Ayr on 2 October 1790, [ABR]; to Antigua in 1791. [NAS.NRAS#3572/2/135]

MUIR, JOHN, a merchant in Antigua, 1790.[NAS.CS16.1.173/412]

MUIR, JOHN, eldest son of Reverend John Muir in St Vigeans, Arbroath, Angus, died in Kingston, Jamaica, on 19 March 1849. [SG#18/1816]

MUIRHEAD, AGNES, widow of Dougald Stewart a merchant in Jamaica, testament confirmed on 8 March 1793 with the Commissariat of Stirling. [NAS]

MUNRO, COLIN, born 1758, late of Grenada, died 18 October 1825. [Greyfriars gravestone, Inverness]

MUNRO, GEORGE, in Antigua 1753. [NAS.CS96/644]

MUNRO, GEORGE, a Customs Officer in Jamaica, second son of Sir Harry Munro of Foulis, died in Kingston, Jamaica, on 22 April 1802. [GM.72.686]

MUNRO, GEORGE GUNN, Grenada, was admitted as a freeman of Inverness in November 1811. [IJ:8.11.1811]

MUNRO, GUN, died in Grenada, 1829. [NAS.GD23.6.655]

MUNRO, HUGH, a prisoner in Edinburgh Tolbooth, indented with John Ramsay a merchant in Glasgow for service in Jamaica(?) on 16 September 1726. [NAS.HH11.15]

MUNRO, HUGH, a surgeon in St Thomas in the Vale, Jamaica, died in Spanish Town, Jamaica, in 1797.
[EWJ#1]

MUNRO, HUGH, born 1750, '45 years resident', died 23 April 1829. [Trinity Chapel gravestone, Green Island, Jamaica]

MUNRO, HUGH, Green Island, Jamaica, 1833.
[NAS.242/70/4/11.Tain]

MUNRO, JAMES, died in Jamaica before February 1792.
[GCr#70]

MUNRO, JOHN, of Alves Kirkton, late of Passage Fort,
Kingston, Jamaica, granted lands of Kirkton of Alves on
20 December 1787. [NAS.RGS.124.201]

MUNRO, W., MBCM, late medical officer of Clackmannan,
married Augusta Ann, eldest daughter of W. B. Baird of
St Kitts, there on 6 February 1868. [S#7675]

MUNRO, WILLIAM, in Jamaica, testament confirmed on 9
November 1809. [NAS.CC16.9.10/237]

MUNRO, WILLIAM, a surgeon in Antigua, 1830.
[NAS.RS.Argyll#1551]

MUNRO, ..., son of W. Munro, was born in St Kitts 20 June
1869. [S#8107]

MURE, HELEN, wife of ......Hunter a merchant in Antigua,
1779. [NAS.CS16.1.175]

MURE, MARGARET, wife of Dr William Bowie a physician in
Antigua, 1779. [NAS.CS16.1.175]

MURE, RICHARD, born in 1830, son of Rupert and Mary, an
engineer, applied to settle in Havana, Cuba, on 7 June
1858. [NAC.Cartas de Domocilio]

MURE, THOMAS, in Warriston, late in Jamaica, was admitted
as a burgess of Edinburgh on 3 November 1790.
[Edinburgh Burgess Roll]

MURRAY, ALEXANDER, born in Rogart, Sutherlandshire,
during 1784, a private of the 93rd Highlanders who
served in St Kitts during 1827-1828. [NAS.RH2.8.97]

MURRAY, ARCHIBALD, from Kincardine, a divinity student in
1826, a teacher in Jamaica, died there in 1844. [AUPC]

MURRAY, GEORGE, born 1729, died 14 April 1804.
[Savanna-la-Mar gravestone, Jamaica]

MURRAY, GEORGE, formerly in Kingston, Jamaica, then in
Savanna la Mar, Jamaica, 1773. [NAS.CS16.1.154/177]

MURRAY, JAMES, married Anne, eldest daughter of Patrick
Waugh, Arbuthnott Cottage, Stirlingshire, and Dromilly
Estate, Trelawney, Jamaica, at Georgia Estate,
Trelawney, Jamaica, on 24 September 1840. [AJ#4848]

MURRAY, PETER, Jamaica, graduated MD from Edinburgh
University in 1802. [EMG#33]

MURRAY, WALTER, Golden Grove Plantation, Jamaica,
1767. [NAS.NRAS#2177/6083]

MURRAY, WILLIAM, born in 1784, son of Alexander Murray
and Catherine McGuffie, died in Jamaica on 22 August
1800. [Wigtown gravestone]

MURRAY, WILLIAM, fifth son of Patrick Murray a writer in
Glasgow, died in Port of Spain, Trinidad, on 3 April
1853. [EEC#22429]

MURRAY, Mrs ...., born 1783, relict of Henry Murray,
Woodbrook, Trinidad, died at the residence of her son
Dr Murray in Port of Spain, Trinidad, on 5 February
1868. [S#7688]

MUSCHET, Dr GEORGE, from British Guina, youngest son of
Richard Muschet a merchant in Dalkeith, Midlothian,
died in St Kitts on 24 March 1860. [S#1517]

MUSCHET, ROBERT, of Green, a merchant in Jamaica,
1778. [NAS.CS16.1.173/400]

NAPIER, MARGARET, eldest daughter of the late Dr Robert
Napier of Grenada and of Bervie in Scotland, died in
Montrose, Angus, on 24 April 1863. [S#2450]

NAPIER, THOMAS, only son of Archibald Napier in St Kitts,
matriculated at Glasgow University in 1796, later a
Cornet of the Dragoons, died during September 1817.
[MAGU#182]

NAPIER, THOMAS, Tobago, graduated MA in Aberdeen on
29 March 1811. [AUL]

NASMYTH, Dr JAMES, a physician in Jamaica, 1778.
[NAS.CS16.1.174]

NASMITH, ROBERT, son of Thomas Nasmith in Jamaica, 1
June 1811. [NAS.RGS.143.39.70]

NEILSON, JOHN, from Glasgow, second son of James B.
Neilson in Queenshill, Kirkcudbright, died in Trinidad on
16 August 1853. [EEC#22488][S.24.9.1853]

NEILSON, THOMAS, St Mary's, Jamaica, son of Thomas
Neilson a merchant in Falkirk, Stirlingshire, 1799.
[NAS.CS18.706.52]; died in Glasgow during February
1800, testament confirmed with the Commissariat of
Glasgow on 1 May 1800. [NAS.CC9.7.77]

NEWAL, ANDREW, a merchant in Westmoreland, Jamaica,
1780. [NAS.CS16.1.179]

NEWHAM, COLIN, born 1784, son of Daniel Newham in
Templeton, died in Clarendon, Jamaica, on 10 January
1804. [CM#12887]

NICOL, ALEXANDER, a laborer at the Mains of Melgund,
Angus, an indentured servant to Sir James Ogilvie of
Inverquharity to serve on Antigua, from the Clyde to
Antigua in 1784. [DCA: H3330]

NICOL, ARCHIBALD, a planter in Tobago, 1800. [GA:T-ARD#13/1]

NICOL, ROBERT, born in Inverness in 1797, late in Jamaica, died in Inverness on 27 February 1844.
[Inverness Chapel Yard gravestone]

NICOLL, GEORGE, of Arthurstone, late in Jamaica, granted lands of Arthurstone on 3 July 1789.
[NAS.RGS.125.158]

NICOLL, JAMES, son of James Nicoll a mason in Dundee, settled in Kingston, Jamaica, admitted as a burgess of Dundee on 15 November 1823. [Dundee Burgess Roll]

NINIAN, ALEXANDER, a merchant in Tortula, 1800. [GA;T-ARD#13/1]

NISBET, DAVID, a merchant in St Kitts, 1776.
[NLS.MS#8793/4]

NISBET, GEORGE, second son of George Nisbet of Cairnhill, Monklands, Lanarkshire, educated at Glasgow University in 1781, died in Westmoreland, Jamaica, on 30 January 1811. [MAGU#132][Caribbeana#4.17]

NISBET, JAMES, in Nevis, 1776. [NLS.Acc.8793/4,32]

NISBET, JAMES, of Letham, born 1737, died in Jamaica on 4 October 1780. [Nisbet of that Ilk, p.208, {London, 1941}]

NISBET, JOSEPH, West Indies, graduated MD at Edinburgh University in 1768. [EMG#9]

NISBET, ROBERT, of Greenholm, born 1730, died in Jamaica on 5 July 1787. [Nisbet of that Ilk, p.208, {London, 1941}]]

NISBET, WALTER, a planter in Nevis, 1777. [NLS.MS#8793]; probate 16 February 1799 PCC

NIVEN, ANDREW, from Alyth, Perthshire, a divinity student in 1828, then a minister in Stirling and later in Jamaica, died 1846. [AUPC]

NOCKELLS, CHARLES, Mount Pleasant, St Thomas in the East, Jamaica, died in Edinburgh on 8 September 1850. [EEC#22015]

OCHTERLONY, DAVID, in Antigua 1757. [DA.Ogilvie pp/21]

OGILVIE, Dr DAVID, a surgeon late of Kingston, Jamaica, now in Aberdeen, 1782. [NAS.CS17.1.1/78]

OGILVIE, FELICITY, born in Carriacou 1782, died 26 May 1831 in Auchenfree, Dunbartonshire. [Cardross gravestone]

OGILVIE, GEORGE, Langley Park, Jamaica, married Barbara Dundas, third daughter of James Dundas of that Ilk, in

Edinburgh on 10 September 1785. [Edinburgh Marriage Register]

OGILVIE, GEORGE, late of Jamaica, then in Dundee, 1800. [DCA:H187]

OGILVIE, JOHN, in Antigua 1761. [DA.Ogilvie.ms.p63]

OGILVIE, THOMAS, in Antigua, 1802. [NAS.GD205.box11/7]

OGILVY, ALEXANDER, died in Jamaica before 1811. [NAS.GD16.Sec.42/227]

OLD, JOHN, a supercargo in the West Indies, 1786. [NAS.CS17.1.5/137]

OLIPHANT, CHARLES, a Jacobite rebel, transported from London to Antigua on the Prince George, master James Nairn, on 14 January 1748, landed 16 March 1748. [NA.T53/44]

ORD, JAMES, planter of 170 acres, St Andrew's parish, Jamaica, 1754. [NA.CO137/28]

ORR, ANDREW, from East Lothian, was admitted as a burgher of St Eustatia, DWI, on 8 August 1781. [NA.CO318.8.83]

ORR, JOHN, Bybrook, St Elizabeth's, Jamaica, 1778. [NLS.MS5332/236]

ORROCK, Captain JOHN, late of the 33rd Regiment, died in Kingston, Jamaica, on 14 February 1838. [AJ#4712]

OSWALD, CATHERINE WHYTE, daughter of James Oswald, superintendent of the Inland Revenue in Elgin, Morayshire, married John Collie, a planter in Couve, at Port of Spain, Trinidad, on 10 December 1860. [S#1743]; wife of john Collie a planter, died on Perseverance Estate, Couva, Trinidad, on 18 September 1863. [S#2600]

PARKER, JOHN, jr., a merchant in Kingston, Jamaica, 1778. [NAS.CS16.1.174]

PASLEY, T. MALCOLM SABINE, Commander of HMS Atalanta, eldest son of Rear Admiral Sir Thomas Sabine Pasley, married Emma Louise Losh, eldest daughter of W. Losh in Trinidad, at Port of Spain, Trinidad, on 13 February 1860. [DC#23486][S#1483]

PATTERSON, FERGUS, in Grenada, 1776. [NLS.Acc8793/30]

PATTERSON, JAMES, a merchant in Cuba, testament 1860 Edinburgh.[NAS.SC70.1.105/465]

PATERSON, JAMES, a surgeon in Dundee, late in Jamaica, 1752. [NAS.RD2.211.2.595]; admitted as a burgess of Edinburgh in 1752. [Edinburgh Burgess Roll]

PATERSON, JAMES, born 1745, second son of Reverend John Paterson and his wife Jean Turing, a physician who died in Jamaica on 25 April 1798. [Coull gravestone]

PATERSON, JOHN, a merchant in St Kitts, 1800. [NAS.CS18.714.25]

PATERSON, W., in Jamaica, dead by 1840. [NAS.GD3.2.144]

PATERSON, WILLIAM, in Jamaica, 1779, son of William Patterson in Easter Frew. [NAS.CS16.1.175]

PATERSON, WILLIAM, an attorney-at-law in Kingston, Jamaica, 1788. [NAS.RS.Argyll#415]

PATERSON, WILLIAM, born in Kilmarnock during 1755, settled in Jamaica, died in Wellington Square, Ayr, on 9 June 1832. [Kilmarnock Laigh gravestone, Ayrshire][ST.VII.490]

PATERSON, WILLIAM, son of Reverend Henry Paterson, Gateside, Dumfries-shire, died in Antigua on 18 July 1843. [EEC#20650]

PATON, JOSEPH, a gentleman in Jamaica, was admitted as a burgess and guildsbrother of Ayr on 4 April 1751. [ABR]

PATTEN, ARCHIBALD, a Jacobite rebel, transported from Liverpool to Jamaica on the Elizabeth, master Daniel Cole, on 7 February 1748, landed 21 March 1748. [NA.T53/44]

PAULL, JOHN ALEXANDER, born in 1842, son of late George Paull of Newseat, Aberdeenshire, died on Calder Estate, St Vincent, on 30 April 1868. [AJ:3.6.1868]

PAULL, THOMAS, born 1777, son of James Paull and Margaret Black, died in Trinidad on 31 December 1803. [St Nicholas gravestone, Aberdeen]

PAXTON, ..., born 1804, Lieutenant Colonel of the 69th Regiment, died in Trinidad on 24 August 1853. [EEC#22489]

PEEBLES, JAMES, son of William Peebles a minister in Ayr, graduated MA from Glasgow University in 1801, 'went to Kingston, Jamaica.' [RGG#494]

PENNYCOOK, ROBERT, in Westmoreland, Cornwall County, Jamaica, died on 13 September 1826, testament

confirmed with the Commissariat of Edinburgh on 1
June 1927. [NAS.CC8.8.151]

PETERSWALD, WILLIAM, in St Mary's, Jamaica, 19 April
1836. [NAS.RS.Edinburgh.45/228]

PETRIE, ALEXANDER, in Antigua, 1778, nephew of
Alexander Petrie a vintner in Elgin, Morayshire.
[NAS.CS16.1.173/357]

PETTIGREW, ALEXANDER, graduated MA from Glasgow
University in 1805, a writer in Glasgow, died in Havanna
during October 1825. [RGG#495]

PHILLIPS, CHARLES H., late of Jamaica, 24 December
1826. [NAS.B2/2.4.60]

PIERSON, Captain, of the Anne died in Jamaica before
February 1792. [GCr#70]

PIRIE, ANDREW, born in Aberdeen during 1797, died in St
Paul's, Antigua, on 22 June 1871. [AJ:2.8.1871]

PIRRY, JAMES, merchant in Trinidad, co-owner of the Maria
of Greenock 1800. [NAS.CE60.11.6/9]

PITCAIRN, ROBERT, St Catherine's parish, Middlesex
County, Jamaica, will 28 July 1778. [NAS.GD1.675.61]

PITCAIRN, ROBERT, tavern keeper in Spanish Town,
Jamaica, 1780s,1792. [NAS.GD1.675.113/135/143]

POLSON, HUGH, son of John Polson and his wife Janet
Mackay in Navidale, the Provost of the Vice Admiralty
Court of Jamaica in 1774. [BM#295]

PORTEOUS, GEORGE, born 11 July 1766 in Glasgow, son of
Reverend William Porteous and his wife Grizel Lindsay,
died in Spring Valley, Jamaica, on 6 December 1793.
[F.3.443]

PORTEOUS, JAMES, born 25 June 1761 in Glasgow, son of
Reverend William Porteous and his wife Grizel Lindsay,
settled in Bonhill, Jamaica. [F.3.443]

POUSTIE, JOHN, a Jacobite rebel, transported from Liverpool
to Jamaica on the Elizabeth, master Daniel Cole, on 7
February 1748, landed 21 March 1748. [NA.T53/44]

PRINGLE, JAMES, in Jamaica, 1765. [NAS.GD18.4206]

PRINGLE, THOMAS, settled in St Paul's parish, Dominica, in
July 1768. [NA.CO142.31]

PRINGLE, WALTER, settled in St Paul's parish, Dominica, in
July 1768. [NA.CO142.31]

PRINGLE, WILLIAM, a surgeon in Antigua, later in Kelso,
Roxburghshire, 1754. [NAS.RS.Edin#143/203]

PURDIE, ROBERT, from Lanark, died on Leogan Estate, Jamaica, on 31 August 1843. [SG.XI.1228]

RADCLIFF, JAMES, indented in Edinburgh for service in Jamaica on 18 March 1741. [CM#3273]

RADCLIFFE, Reverend J., minister of the Church of Scotland, Kingston, Jamaica, married Isabella Cooke, eldest daughter of A. D. Cooke, MD, Custos of the parish of St Mary, in Green Park, St Ann's, Jamaica, 29 January 1862. [S#2106]

RAEBURN, JAMES, born 1822, on of Reverend Gordon Raeburn, schoolmaster at Keig, Aberdeenshire, manager of Lavington's Estate in Antigua, died 17 June 1851. [AJ#5399]

RAIT, JAMES, from Glasgow, died at Montego Bay on 28 December 1841. [GSP#705]

RAITT, ANDREW, planter of 60 acres, St Andrew's parish, Jamaica, 1754. [NA.CO137/28]

RALSTON, JOHN, a merchant in Jamaica, 1813, grandson of Duncan Clyde a cooper in Campbeltown, Argyll. [NAS.RS.Argyll#2329]

RAMSAY, GEORGE, Jacobite rebel, transported from London to Antigua on the Prince George on 14 January 1748, landed 16 March 1748. [NA.T53/44]; in Antigua, 1760. [DA.Ogilvie.ms.p46]

RAMSAY, MARY, in Jamaica before 1738. [Island Record Office, Jamaica, Attorney, #29.2-7/204]

RAMSAY, ROBERT, jr., from Dumfries, emigrated to the West Indies in 1796. [NAS.GD45.14.533]

RAMSAY, ROBERT, a superintendent and chief engineer, died in Nassau, New Providence, on 3 August 1809. [PC#56]

RANKINE, DONALD, in Tobago, dead by 1822. [NAS.CS17.1.41/604]

RATCLIFF, JAMES, indented for Jamaica on 18 March 1741. [CM#3273]

RATTRAY, JOHN, [Jan Rattery], a widower, born in Scotland, settled on St Martin, DWI, married Catherina Simons, widow of Lucas Raapzaat, born on Saba but resident of St Eustatia, there on 21 June 1734. ['Afscriften huwelijkakten van St Eustatius van 1710-1750']

RATTRAY, JOHN, eldest son of Thomas Rattray, merchant, and Janet Marshall, a merchant in Jamaica 1763-. [GA.B10.15.7056]

REDDIE, ANDREW, died in Lucea, Jamaica, on 15 February 1820. [GkAd#2393]

REED, GEORGE, youngest son of George Reed, Hallcross House, Fisherrow, Musselburgh, died in St Kitts on 12 September 1860. [S#1663]

REID, ADAM, born in Aberdeen 1795, died on Mount Desire, Carriacou, by Grenada, on 21 February 1867. [S#7395]

REID, ISABELLA JANE, widow of Commander John Reid RN, died at Bunker's Hill, Jamaica, on 20 January 1878. [EC#29151]

REID, JOHN, a merchant in Curacao, 1779. [NAS.CS16.1.175]

REID, JOHN, a planter on Carriacou, the Grenadines, 1780. [NAS.CS16.1.179]

REID, MARK HORNE, youngest son of Robert Reid a surgeon in Antigua, matriculated at Glasgow University in 1802, graduated MD in 1803. [MAGU#202]

REID, ROBERT SAMUEL, born in Antigua, eldest son of Robert Reid MD, matriculated at Glasgow University in 1791, a surgeon who died in Antigua on 16 September 1804. [MAGU#165]

REID, THOMAS, in Dundee, formerly a merchant in Jamaica, son of Thomas Reid of Drumgeith, a merchant baillie of Dundee, 1766. [NAS.RS35.16.XXI.439]; 1770, [DCA: H1906/1916]

REID, THOMAS, a merchant in Jamaica, 1779. [NAS.CS16.1.75]

REID, THOMAS, from Ayrshire, was admitted as a burgher of St Eustatia, DWI, on 8 August 1780. [NA.CO318.8.83]

REID, WILLIAM, son of Dr Andrew Reid, 95 South Portland Street, Glasgow, died at Montego Bay, Jamaica, on 15 December 1841. [GSP#705]

REID, Reverend WILLIAM, minister of Borgue, married Anna Tomlinson, third daughter of John Robert Tomlinson of Huntly, in Huntly, Manchester, Jamaica, on 16 June 1849. [SG#18/1832]

RENNY, ALEXANDER, of Borrowfield, eldest son of Robert Renny a merchant in Jamaica, granted the lands of Borrowfield on 21 December 1795. [NAS.RGS.128.148]

RENNY, JAMES, a planter in Jamaica, 1780. [NLS#8794]

RENNY, ROBERT, late of Jamaica, then of Montrose, 1787. [GA.TD219/6]

RENNICK, ALEXANDER, eldest son of William Rennick a merchant in Jamaica, matriculated at Glasgow University in 1811. [MAGU#258]

REYNALLS, EDWARD, from Jamaica, an apprentice surgeon, died in Edinburgh on 6 September 1751. [AJ#194]

RICH, ANDREW, died at Mount Rich, Grenada, on 27 November 1779. [Glasgow Mercury#III.115]

RICHMOND, WALTER, a merchant in Kingston, Jamaica, 1770. [NAS.RD4.211.55]

RICHMOND, WILLIAM, born 16 July 1780 in Irvine, Ayrshire, son of Reverend James Richmond and his wife Margaret Cunningham, died in Jamaica on 25 June 1796. [F.3.100]

RIDDELL, JAMES, late in Grenada then in Ayr, was admitted as a burgess and guilds-brother of Ayr on 27 July 1776. [ABR]

RIDDELL, JAMES, a merchant in Guadaloupe, 1782. [NAS.CS17.1.1/97]

RIDDELL, WALTER, Bermuda, graduated MD at Edinburgh University in 1774. [EMG#12]

RITCHIE, ALEXANDER, merchant in Nassau, New Providence, co-owner of the Omoa of Glasgow, 1797, the Good Intent of Greenock, 1798; the George of Glasgow, 1799; the Margaret of Glasgow, 1799; the Crowe Isle of Glasgow, 1800; the Montezuma of Glasgow, 1801. [NAS.CE60.11.4/26; 5/62; 6/13/30/31; 7/58]

RITCHIE, ALEXANDER, jr. merchant in Nassau, New Providence, co-owner of the Hunter of Glasgow, 1799. [NAS.CE60.11.7.103]

RITCHIE, EWING, a merchant in Kingston, Jamaica, 1806. [NAS.CS96, CS235, Seqn.C2/2]

RITCHIE, IRVING, merchant in Nassau, New Providence, co-owner of the Omoa of Glasgow, 1797; the Good Intent of Glasgow, 1798. [NAS.CE60.11.4/26; 5/62]

RITCHIE, JOHN, merchant in Nassau, New Providence, co-owner of the Omoa of Glasgow, 1797; the Good Intent of Glasgow, 1798; the Margaret of Glasgow 1799. [NAS.CE60.11.4/26; 5/62; 6/19]

RITCHIE, ROBERT, from Fife, was admitted as a burgher of St Eustatia, DWI, on 21 November 1780. [NA.CO318.8.84v]

RIVERS, SHADLOCK, born in St Kitts, fifth son of Shadlock
Rivers a merchant, matriculated at Glasgow University
in 1794. [MAGU#177]

ROBB, Miss, died in Brownberry, St Elizabeth's, Jamaica, on
31 March 1805. [CM#13073]

ROBB, WILLIAM, of Duthieston, residing in Jamaica, eldest
son of John Robb the Sheriff of Dunblane, granted lands
in Dunblane on 2 June 1818. [NAS.RGS.157.46.102]

ROBERTSON, ALEXANDER, late of Jamaica, husband of
Margaret Farquharson of Alrick, 1779,
[NAS.CS16.1.175]; 1788. [NAS.GD16.11.32]

ROBERTSON, ALEXANDER, born 1793, '28 years in
Jamaica', died at Hillside Pen, St David's, Jamaica, on
18 March 1837. [AJ#4661]

ROBERTSON, CHARLES, died in Jamaica before February
1792. [GCr#70]

ROBERTSON, DANIEL, eldest son of Captain Daniel
Robertson of Calcutta, India, died in Fourpaths,
Clarendon, Jamaica, on 27 March 1849. [SG#18/1819]

ROBERTSON, DAVID, a saddler in Jamaica, 1835.
[NAS.SC70.1.50.333]

ROBERTSON, DUNCAN, born 1 January 1780, son of Rev.
James Robertson minister of Callander, Perthshire, and
his wife Isabella Graham, settled in Jamaica. [F.4.340]

ROBERTSON, FRANCIS, attorney at law in Kingston,
Jamaica, 1792. [NAS.CS17.1.11/7]; in Jamaica 1805.
[AUL.ms3175/206]

ROBERTSON, HARRY, of Newton, formerly in Havannah, 6
October 1838. [NAS.RS.Nairn.4/117]

ROBERTSON, HENRY, a planter in Jamaica, 1780.
[NLS.MS#8794]

ROBERTSON, JAMES, born 11 March 1769, son of George
Robertson and his wife Ann Allan in Aberdeen,
educated at King's College, Aberdeen, 1786-1790, then
a surgeon in Jamaica. [KCA.2.366]

ROBERTSON, JAMES, in Jamaica, was admitted as a
burgess of Banff in 1783. [Banff Burgess Roll]

ROBERTSON, JAMES, Jamaica, married Maria Innes,
youngest daughter of Alexander Innes of Cathlaw on 4
March 1789. [AJ]

ROBERTSON, JAMES, late in Jamaica, testament 31 August
1816 [NAS.CC16.9.11,283]

ROBERTSON, JAMES, late in Jamaica, now in Kelso, Roxburghshire, 1821. [NAS.CC18.4.5.82-108]

ROBERTSON, JANE, second daughter of Allan Robertson in Nassau, New Providence, married H. H. Munro, secretary of the Stock Exchange, in Glasgow on 24 April 1848. [SG#17/1712]

ROBERTSON, JOHN, a prisoner in Edinburgh Tolbooth indented with John Ramsay for service in Jamaica (?) on 13 September 1726. [NAS.HHII.15]

ROBERTSON, JOHN, in Jamaica, 11 November 1760. [NAS.RH1.2.977]

ROBERTSON, JOHN, gentleman on Green Island, Jamaica, 1783. [NAS.CS17.1.2/217]

ROBERTSON, JOHN, in Kingston, Jamaica, died 1807, testament Edinburgh 1836. [NAS.CC8.11.7.116]

ROBERTSON, MARGARET, in Antigua, 1753. [NAS.CS96/645]

ROBERTSON, Hon. PETER, St Thomas in the East, Jamaica, 1821. [NAS.SC49.48.25.16/252; GD132.159, 160]

ROBERTSON, WILLIAM, a surgeon in Jamaica, husband of Agnes Norrie, 1773. [NAS.CS16.1.154/122]

ROBERTSON, WILLIAM, St Ann's, Jamaica, admitted as a burgess of Nairn on 8 August 1776. [NAS.GD2.132]

ROBISON, Dr GEORGE, Hospital Staff, died at Fort Charlotte, Lucea, Jamaica, on 7 January 1804. [CM#121875]

ROBISON, WALTER, late in Clarendon, Jamaica, 1773. [NAS.CS16.1.154/186]

ROBISON, WILLIAM, servant of William Salmon in Antigua, was admitted as a burgess and guilds-brother of Ayr on 5 February 1757. [ABR]

ROCHEAD, JOHN, a merchant in Jamaica, was admitted as a burgess of Glasgow in 1719. [Glasgow Burgess Roll]

RODGER, WILLIAM, assistant surgeon in the Royal Navy, son of deacon James Rodger in Ayr, died in Grenada during October 1838. [SG#8/769]

ROLLAND, PATRICK, born 1798, second son of Patrick Rolland in Montrose, died in Jamaica on 22 January 1820. [MC#28]

ROME, JOHN, in Jamaica, eldest son of Peter Rome in Redkirk, 1782. [NAS.CS17.1.40/32]

ROME, THOMAS, a merchant in Antigua, 1715, 1719,
[NAS.GD78.208; GD135.1615]

ROSE, CHARLES, a minister in Antigua, Depute Judge of the
Admiralty Court there, graduated Doctor of Law at King's
College, Aberdeen, on 28 January 1748.[Fasti
Aberdonenses, Aberdeen 1854, fo.447]; in Antigua
1753. [NAS.CS96/644]

ROSE, JOHN, born 1810, son of Alexander Rose [1767-1846]
and Mary Clark [1773-1850] in Summerfield, died 15
November 1838 in Treadways Estate, St Thomas in the
Vale, Jamaica. [Alloway gravestone, Ayrshire]

ROSE, Mr, from Jamaica, buried in St Nicholas churchyard,
Aberdeen, 25 December 1788. [ACA]

ROSE, Dr ...., from Nairn, a physician in Jamaica, 1808.
[NAS.GD171.914]

ROSS, Mr ALEXANDER, son of John Ross, late of Jamaica,
buried in St Nicholas churchyard, Aberdeen, 1 July
1778. [ACA]

ROSS, CHARLES, a merchant in Antigua, 1794.
[ECA.Moses#172/6745]

ROSS, CHARLES, master of the Emerald Isle, fourth son of
Charles Ross in Cromarty, died in Matantas 15 October
1861. [S#1986]

ROSS, DANIEL, a merchant in Nevis, 1778.
[NAS.CS16.1.173/434]

ROSS, G. C., second son of Alexander Ross in Morham,
Haddington, died at Aux Cayes, Haiti, on 24 November
1866. [S#7308]

ROSS, HERCULES, in Jamaica, admitted as a burgess and
guilds-brother of Glasgow on 9 October 1782, [GBR]; of
Rossie, late in Jamaica, granted the lands of Rossie on
3 July 1784. [NAS.RGS.122.138]

ROSS, JOHN, a prisoner in Edinburgh Tolbooth indented with
John Ramsay a merchant in Glasgow for service in
Jamaica, September 1726. [NAS.HH11.15]

ROSS, Captain JOHN, in Antigua 1758. [DA.Ogilvie pp/28]

ROSS, JOHN, in Jamaica, 1760. [NAS.RH1.2.977]

ROSS, JOHN, a merchant late of Tobago, died at the Cove of
Cork on 8 February 1781. [GM#IV/78]

ROSS, JOHN, second son of Zaechei Ross of Hawk, a
gentleman in St Thomas, matriculated at Glasgow
University in 1804, graduated MD in 1811. [MAGU#209]

ROSS, JOHN, of Scarpoe, jr., died in Cuba, 1818.
[NAS.CC17.5.6. ff213-5]

ROSS, JOHN, born 1806, son of Alexander Ross (1725-1782) a flesher in Aberdeen, and Susannah Johnston (1724-1795), died in Tobago 3 August 1826. [St Peter's, Spittal, Aberdeen, gravestone]

ROSS, JOHN, born 1778, son of Alexander Ross (1737-1783) and Margaret Udny (1732-1819), died at Clark's Court, Grenada, on 26 September 1833. [St Nicholas gravestone, Aberdeen]

ROSS, Dr JOHN, from Edinburgh, died at Montego Bay, Jamaica, on 2 September 1863. [S#2588]

ROSS, Mrs MARGARET, St Mary's, Jamaica, 1807. [NAS.GD417.211]

ROSS, PATRICK, a hairdresser in Kingston, Jamaica, 1829. [NAS.SC48.49.25.27/74]

ROSS, WILLIAM, born 1741, son of James Ross and his wife Agnes Dunn in Mill of Towtie, died in Jamaica during 1798. [Fetteresso gravestone]

ROSS, WILLIAM, a merchant at Port Maria Bay, St Mary's, Jamaica, 1780. [NAS.CS16.1.179]

ROSS, WILLIAM, a merchant in Jamaica, son of David Ross in Roslin, 1783. [NAS.CS17.1.2/257]

ROSS, Dr., in Jamaica, 1760. [NAS.RH1.2.977]

ROY, ANDREW, born 1845, died in St Vincent 29 July 1877. [Straiton gravestone, Ayrshire]

RUAN, WILLIAM, eldest son of William Ruan a merchant in Santa Cruz [St Croix?], matriculated at Glasgow University in 1810, graduated MD from Edinburgh University in 1818, married Christine Dumbreck from Edinburgh, in St Croix on 16 February 1824, died in St Croix on 29 November 1857. [MAGU#249][EMG#57]

RUSSEL, DAVID, JP, second son of David Russel in St Andrews, died on Mesopotamia Estate, Jamaica, in 1867. [S#7485]

RUSSEL, ROBERT, JP, eldest son of David Russel in St Andrews, Fife, died on Dry River Estate, Jamaica, on 5 August 1867. [S#7514]

RUSSELL, WILLIAM, a planter in Tobago, died 1790. [NAS.GD44.34.46.1]

RUSSELL, WILLIAM G., book-keeper in Jamaica, 1883. [NAS.RS.Kirkcaldy.22.57]

RUTHERFORD, JOHN, a surgeon in Antigua, son of Thomas Rutherford a merchant in Edinburgh, 1744. [NAS.CS16.1.75]

RUTHVEN, JANE MIDDLETON, from Cults Farm, Galloway, died on Good Intent, Westmoreland, Jamaica, 1853.[S.9.4.1853]

RYEBURN, JOHN, in St George, Grenada, co-owner of the Pomona of Glasgow and of the Alfred of Glasgow, 1798, the Nancy of Greenock 1805. [NAS.CE60.11.5/71/108; 8/63]

RYEBURN, THOMAS, in Jamaica, co-owner of the Pomona of Glasgow and of the Alfred of Glasgow, 1798, [NAS.CE60.11.5/71/108]

SADDLER, JAMES, a merchant in St Kitts now in Bristol 1782. [NAS.CS17.1.1/37]

SALMON, WILLIAM, in Antigua 1757. [DA.Ogilvie pp/23]; was admitted as a burgess and guilds-brother of Ayr on 5 February 1757. [ABR]

SAMUELS, PAUL STEVEN, born 1774, Negril Spots, Jamaica, died 18 November 1850. [Dean gravestone, Edinburgh]

SANDERS, WILLIAM, from Closeburn, Dumfriesshire, died in Trinidad during 1817. [S#22]

SANG, WILLIAM, son of William Sang a baker in Aberdeen, settled in Tobago before 1828. [St Nicholas gravestone, Aberdeen]

SAUNDERS, JAMES, born 1795, son of Alexander Saunders in Banff, died in Jamaica on 3 September 1811. [Banff gravestone]

SAUNDERS, ROBERT, shipbuilder late of Antigua, 21 October 1796. [NAS.SC20.36.17]

SAVAGE, GEORGE, in Antigua, 1753. [NAS.CS96/645]

SAWERS, ALEXANDER, in Jamaica, 1773. [NAS.CS16.1.154]

SCARLETT, Sir WILLIAM, Chief Justice of Jamaica, died there on 10 October 1831, [PA#124]

SCOLLAY, JOHN, a merchant in Kingston, Jamaica, 1800. [NAS.CS17.1.19/179]

SCOTT, AUGUSTA MARY, wife of Frederick John Scott, died in Port of Spain, Trinidad, on 18 January 1862. [S#2082]

SCOTT, DAVID, applied to settle in Havana, Cuba, on 22 October 1856. [NAC.Cartas de Domocilio]

SCOTT, EBENEZER, MD, surgeon on <u>HMS Cornwallis</u>, died in Port Royal, Jamaica, on 30 December 1838. [AJ#4755]

SCOTT, Mrs ELIZABETH, born 1828, wife of Reverend John Scott, died at Montego Bay, Jamaica, 15 November 1848. [West Linton gravestone, Peebles-shire]

SCOTT, FRANCIS CARTERET, at Montego Bay 1787. [NAS.GD237/9/4/9]; the Customs Collector at Montego Bay, Jamaica, married Charlotte Elizabeth Cunningha, eldest daughter of Colonel Cunningham of the Scots Brigade, in 1801. [GM.71.11051]

SCOTT, GEORGE, in Kinloss, Jamaica, granted the lands of Woodend, Roxburgh, on 20 December 1836. [NAS.RGS.212.5]

SCOTT, HELEN, born 1844, from Edinburgh, wife of William Miller, Santa Margarita Estate, Trinidad, died 6 January 1870. [S#8273]

SCOTT, HENRY ELLIOT, born 1847, late of the Electric Tile Company of Edinburgh, died in Trinidad on 30 November 1869. [S#8247]

SCOTT, JAMES, from Comieston, died in Jamaica on 14 October 1801. [GM.72.83]

SCOTT, JAMES, born in Dundee on 6 June 1786, son of Reverend James Scott and his wife Margaret Munro, settled in Jamaica, died 12 December 1824. [F.5.310]

SCOTT, JOAN, daughter of George Scott and his spouse Isobel Pott, Jamaica, 1779. [NAS.CS16.1.175]

SCOTT, JOHN, planter of 604 acres, St Andrew's parish, Jamaica, 1754. [NA.CO137/28]

SCOTT, Reverend JOHN, of the United Presbyterian Congregation at Montego Bay, Jamaica, died there on 4 December 1848. [SG#18/1784]; born 1820, son of Andrew Scott and Janet Penman, died at Montego Bay 4 December 1848. [West Linton gravestone, Peebles-shire]

SCOTT, LOUISA, wife of Archibald Scott, Falmouth, Jamaica, formerly in Greenock, died in Bath, St Thomas in the East, Jamaica, on 22 November 1843. [GEP#839]

SCOTT, Mrs MARY, daughter of George Scott, late of Jamaica, died in Edinburgh on 22 February 1789. [GM#XII.578.38]

SCOTT, WALTER, eldest son of Walter D. Scott in Edinburgh, married Amelie, eldest daughter of Charles Miot a

merchant in Haiti, in Port au Prince on 17 February
1868. [S#7684]

SCOTT, WILLIAM HENRY, a merchant in St Eustatius, son of
Alexander Scott a merchant in Edinburgh, died in
Antigua on 12 May 1789. [GM#XII.601.212]

SCOTT, Mr..., emigrated from Greenock to Jamaica on the
Mary of Glasgow on 29 November 1773.
[NAS.CE60.1.7]

SCOTT, ..., son of Archibald Scott, was born in Antigua on 22
December 1859. [W#21/2161]

SCOTT, ..., son of Walter Scott, was born at Port au Prince,
Haiti, on 12 November 1868. [S#7923]

SCRYMGEOUR, HENRY, late of Jamaica, youngest son of
David Scrymgeour of Birkhill, 1793. [NAS.NRAS#783/9];
married Mary Turner Maitland, daughter of Captain
Frederick Maitland of Rankeillor, in Edinburgh on 3 April
1793. [Edinburgh Marriage Register]

SEATON, HENRY, in St Kitts, 1776. [NLS.Acc8793/21]

SEATON, HENRY, born in Scotland, a merchant in the West
Indies, a Lieutenant of Diemens Hussars 1781.
[NA.CO5/Vol.III]

SHAND, FRANCIS, born in Kemnay, Aberdeenshire, on 2
August 1786, second son of Reverend John Shand and
his wife Margaret Dauney, educated at King's College,
Aberdeen, from 1799 to 1803, an advocate who died in
Spanish town, Jamaica, on 10 March 1827.
[KCA.2.385][SAA

SHAND, JOHN, in Spanish Town, Jamaica, granted the lands
of Arnhall on 2 June 1815. [NAS.RGS.151.6]

SHAND, WILLIAM, in Spanish Town, Jamaica, granted the
lands of Balmakewan on 2 June 1824.
[NAS.RGS.170.25]; cf William Shand of Arnhall, an
estate manager in Jamaica 1791 to 1823, later a
merchant in Scotland. [NAS.CS46.1852]

SHAND,......, daughter of William Shand of Balmakewan,
was born on Hopewell Plantation, St Ann's, Jamaica, on
5 September 1825. [Blackwood's Magazine#XVIII.779]

SHANNON, ARCHIBALD, born in 1835, son of Archibald
Campbell Shannon a merchant in Jamaica, died in
Maxwell Valley, Falmouth, Jamaica, on 26 December
1838. [SG#8/745]

SHARP, JOHN, in Trelawney, Jamaica, 12 October 1860.
[NAS.RS.Nairn.7/63]

SHAW, ALEXANDER, a bookseller, late of Turnbull and Shaw in Virginia, then in Kingston, Jamaica, February 1789. [NAS.CS17.1.7/90]

SHAW, ALEXANDER, eldest son of Reverend John Shaw in Greenock, educated at Glasgow University in 1766, died in Jamaica on 10 August 1804. [Caribbeana.4.15][GM.74.1071]

SHAW, ALEXANDER, in Jamaica, testament 1869 Edinburgh. [NAS.SC70.1.145/356]

SHAW, DAVID, St Mary's parish, Jamaica, testament 17 March 1812 Edinburgh. [NAS.CC8.11.VI/345]

SHAW, JAMES, Jamaica, was admitted as a burgess of Edinburgh in 1763. [Edinburgh Burgess Roll]

SHAW, JAMES, late of Montserrat, granted the lands of Preston on 6 August 1777. [NAS.RGS.117.241][NAS.RS27.219.33]

SHAW, JAMES, in Jamaica 1842. [NAS.NRAS#0050/43]

SHEARER, JOSEPH, Drax Hall estate, Jamaica, married Elizabeth Jane, eldest daughter of Peter Stuart, Birchbank, at Birchbank, Craigellachie, on 5 January 1876. [AJ#6679]

SHEARER, WILLIAM, born in 1820, son of John and Anne, an engineer, applied to settle in Matanzas, Cuba, on 12 September 1857. [NAC.Cartas de Domocilio]

SHERIFF, ALEXANDER, possibly from Aberdeen, a surveyor in St Mary's, Jamaica, probate 10 March 1802 PCC

SHERIFF, JOHN, in Antigua 1757. [DA.Ogilvie pp/19]

SHERIFF, ROBERT, eldest son of Robert Sheriff a merchant in Glasgow and London, educated at Glasgow University 1819, a merchant in New York, died on Diamond Estate, St Croix, on 18 August 1847. [ANY.2.183]

SHIRREFF, ROBERT P., to Jamaica 1803. [NAS.NRAS#8/23/15]

SILVER, ALEXANDER, sometime in Jamaica, dead by 1797. [NAS.GD70.220]

SIMPSON, ALEXANDER, Baron of the Exchequer in Grenada, granted lands of Auchenleck on 23 February 1771. [NAS.RGS.111.140]

SIMPSON, ALEXANDER, son of Reverend Alexander Simpson in New Machar, Aberdeen, educated at King's College, Aberdeen, from 1812 to 1820, settled in Jamaica. [KCA.2.426]

SIMPSON, JAMES, in Antigua 1757. [DA.Ogilvie pp/15]

SIMSON, JAMES, in Grenada, 1776. [NLS.Acc8793/13]; a merchant in Glasgow then in Grenada, 1780. [NAS.CS16.1.177]

SIMSON, JOHN, naval officer at St Vincent, 1772. [NAS.CS16.1.151/48]

SINCLAIR, DAVID, in Jamaica, 1719. [NAS.GD164.545]

SINCLAIR, EDWARD, SSC, from Edinburgh, died at the house of David Cooper, Mount Pleasant, Jamaica, on 22 March 1840. [EEC#20055]

SINCLAIR, JAMES, in Jamaica, possibly from Canisby, Caithness, 1808. [NAS.GD139.390.2]

SINCLAIR, JOHN, assistant surgeon on HMS Pylades, son of D. Smith in Kinloch Rannoch, died in Jamaica during August 1825. [Blackwood's Magazine#XVIII.779]

SINCLAIR, JOHN, a baker from Glasgow, died at Montego Bay, Jamaica, on 31 August 1843. [SG.XI.1239]

SINCLAIR, KENNEDY, in Jamaica, 1772. [NAS.CS16.1.148/340]

SINCLAIR, WILLIAM, at Martha Brae, Jamaica, 1812. [NAS.SC48.49.25.5/200]

SKENE, Dr JAMES, a physician in South Carolina 1767 to 1778, Loyalist, settled in Kingston, Jamaica. [NA.AO12.52.163]

SMAIL, JAMES, of Overmains, late in Jamaica, granted lands of Overmains on 3 February 1786. [NAS.RGS.123.162]

SMART, ADAM, in Antigua, 1758. [NAS.GD219/289]

SMITH, ALEXANDER, in Jamaica, 1757. [NAS.CS16.1.99/122]

SMITH, DAVID, died at Hampstead Park, Kingston, Jamaica, on 6 February 1869. [S#7985]

SMITH, J., Stony Hill, Jamaica, 1785. [NAS.GD190/3/332]

SMITH, JOHN, ('Jan Schmit'), born in 'Ba....', Scotland, a mariner, Johanna Davidts, a widow from St Martin, in St Eustatia on 9 November 1745. ['Afscriften huwelijksakten van St Eustatius van 1710-1750']

SMITH LEWIS LUDOVICK, from Forres, Morayshire, then in Antigua later in St Kitts, 1821. [NAS.CS17.1.40/252]

SMITH, ROBERT, in Kingston, Jamaica, co-owner of the Nancy of Glasgow, 1805. [NAS.CE60.11.8/63]

SNELL, ELIZABETH, wife of Reverend John Scott, died at Montego Bay, Jamaica, on 15 November 1848. [SG#18/1784]

SNODGRASS, HUGH, eldest son of Hugh Snodgrass a writer in Paisley, educated at Glasgow University in 1784, a merchant from Glasgow, in Blue Mountain Valley, Jamaica, 1815, died in Port Royal, Jamaica, on 24 October 1819. [NAS.SC58.42.6.94][MAGU#140] [NAS.NRAS#2654/1/10][Caribeanna#4.17]

SOMERVILLE, JAMES, planter at Forrest Estate, Westmoreland parish, Cornwall County, Jamaica, eldest son of John Somerville of Jenlaw, tenant in Hillhouse, husband of May or Marion Shiells, Whittleknow near Spotswood, Westruther. Process of Divorce, 1794, Commissariat of Edinburgh.

SPALDING, CHARLES ANTHONY, born 1825, fourth son of Hinton Spalding MD, FRCS, Custos Rotulorum of St Andrews, Jamaica, Commissioner of Stamps for Jamaica, died at Nether Arthurlie the home of his uncle Henry Dunlop, 29 August 1861. [S#1939]

SPALDING, COLIN ALEXANDER, fifth son of Hinton Spalding MD in Kingston, Jamaica, died at The Pen, Halfway Tree, Jamaica, on 28 May 1863. [S#2510]

SPALDING, HELEN, second daughter of Hinton Spalding MD, Kingston, Jamaica, wife of William R. Myers, died in Westfield, Spanish Town, Jamaica, on 22 October 1863. [S#2627]

SPALDING, HINTON, Jamaica, graduated MD from Edinburgh University in 1802. [EMG#40]

SPALDING, HINTON, born 1790, an MD in Kingston, Jamaica, died in Bremen, Germany, on 2 June 1853. [EEC#22463]

SPALDING, STEWART, a planter in Jamaica, married Ann Spalding, daughter of Charles Spalding a confectioner, in Edinburgh on 28 July 1796. [Edinburgh Marriage Register]

SPALDING, WILLIAM SHAND, born 1811, third son of Dr Hinton Spalding in Jamaica, died on Mount Atlas, Jamaica, on 10 July 1839. [SG#8/799]

SPARK, WILLIAM, St Thomas parish, Surrey, Jamaica, will subscribed 1 January 1764, probate 25 August 1767 Westmoreland County, Virginia

SPENCE, GEORGE, Jamaica, graduated MD from Edinburgh University in 1790. [EMG#22]

SPENCER, THOMAS, second son of John Spencer a merchant in Jamaica, matriculated at Glasgow University in 1793. [MAGU#173]

SPIER, ANDREW, of Marshyland, Beith, died in Santa Cruz, West Indies, 1852. [S.7.4.1852]

SPINK, MARGARET, born in Scotland, settled in St Eustatia, DWI, married (1) Theophilius Lengton from Saba, in St Eustatia in 1730, (2) Nathaniel Clee from London, in St Eustatia in 1733. ['Afscriften huwelijksakten van St Eustatius van 1710-1750']

SPOTTISWOOD, JAMES, a merchant in Jamaica, married Barbara Sim, daughter of James Sim a writer, in Edinburgh on 25 February 1753. [Edinburgh Marriage Register]

SPOTTISWOOD, JAMES, of Dunnipace, late a merchant in Jamaica, granted lands of Dunnipace on 6 August 1756. [NAS.RGS.103.161][NAS.GD1.529.255]

SPROTT, JOHN, from Greenock to the West Indies in 1812. [NAS.GD171.1019]

SPROTT, MARY ANN, eldest daughter of William Sprott in St Vincent, died in Bruges, Belgium, on 6 February 1870. [S#8283]

STALKER, DUNCAN, late in Tobago then in Killean, Argyll, edict of executry, 1798. [NAS.CC2.8.102, 7]

STARRAT, ROBERT, sometime of Carriacou, Grenada, 1829. [NAS.RS54.5279]

STEEDMAN, ALEXANDER, born in Edinburgh, son of Reverend John Steedman and his wife Jean Kinnaird, died in Jamaica during October 1735. [F.1.140]

STEEL, ALEXANDER, in Jamaica, 1850. [NAS,RD5.868.518]

STEEL, Dr JAMES, born 1821, son of Alexander Steel in Morningside, Edinburgh, died in Oroprouche, West Indies, on 17 December 1846. [EEC#2154]

STEEL, MARY, daughter of Dr John Steel in Jamaica, married Louis Ruffen, a manufacturer in Edinburgh, there on 16 April 1790. [Edinburgh Marriage Register]

STEEL, WILLIAM, born in 1842, son of William Steel a slater in Banff, died at Key West Hospital, Bahamas, on 7 October 1865. [AJ:22.3.1865]

STENHOUSE, WILLIAM, Lieutenant of HMS Jason died at St John's Harbour, Antigua, on 13 June 1805. [CM#13094]

STEPHEN, GEORGE, Grand Pauvre, Diamond Estate, Grenada, 1785. [NAS.GD58.1.16/426]

STEPHEN, JOSEPH, born 1 January 1797 in Fordoun, Kincardineshire, son of Alexander Stephen, farmer of the Mains of Glenfarquhar, and his wife Isabel Robertson, died in Jamaica on 15 January 1821. [Fordoun gravestone]

STEPHEN, Mrs, relict of Reverend John Stephen, DD, New Providence, Bahamas, died in London on 28 February 1839. [AJ#4756]

STEPHENSON, MARY FENTON, wife of William Turner, died in Wallingford, St Elizabeth's, Jamaica, on 17 June 1838. [SG#7/716]

STEVEN, WILLIAM, from Falkirk, Stirlingshire, died in San Fernando, Trinidad, on 25 September 1840. [W#97]

STEVENSON, ALEXANDER, merchant in Nassau, New Providence, co-owner of the <u>Montezuma of Glasgow</u>, 1801. [NAS.CE60.11.7/58]

STEVENSON, ELIZABETH, daughter of Hamilton Stevenson in Jamaica, married John Stirling a grocer, in Edinburgh on 15 January 1796. [Edinburgh Marriage Register]

STEVENSON, HUGH, in Antigua, was admitted as a burgess and guilds-brother of Ayr on 4 June 1783. [ABR]

STEVENSON, JAMES, born in Glasgow on 29 March 1767, son of Nathaniel Stevenson a merchant, educated at Glasgow University in 1779, died in Jamaica. [MAGU#126][Caribeanna#4.15]

STEWART, ALEXANDER, late a merchant at the Bridge of Tilt, Perthshire, now in the West Indies, 1795. [NAS.CS17.1.14/247]

STEWART, Lieutenant ALEXANDER ECKSTEIN, RN, eldest son of Colonel Alexander Stewart, RA, married Belinda, second daughter of Thomas Williams of Nassau, Bahamas, there on 11 January 1877. [EC#28831]

STEWART, ANGUS, a prisoner in Edinburgh Tolbooth, indented with John Ramsay a merchant in Glasgow for service in Jamaica (?) 13 September 1726. [NAS.HH11.15]

STEWART, ARCHIBALD, a merchant in Rotterdam, later in Tobago, 1778. [NAS.CS16.1.173/313]

STEWART, ARCHIBALD, died in Jamaica before February 1792. [GCr#70]

STEWART, CHARLES, fifth son of Charles Stewart of Redshiel and his wife Isobel Haldane, died in Jamaica during 1767. ["Stewarts of Appin"]

STEWART, DANIEL, in St Elizabeth's, Jamaica, 1771.
[NLS.MS5320]

STEWART, DAVID, of Garth, Perthshire, Major General, later
Governor of St Lucia, died in December 1829.
[NAS.GD2.147]

STEWART, DUNCAN, in Clarendon, Jamaica, 1797.
[NAS.NRAS#2654/2/6]

STEWART, ESTHER NESS, born 1815, died at Williams Villa,
Trinidad, 21 December 1844. [Edinburgh, New Calton
gravestone]

STEWART, HOUSTOUN, a planter on Roxburgh Estate,
Tobago, 1836. [NA.T71/1572]

STEWART, JAMES, in Spanish Town, Jamaica, 1815.
[NAS.SC49.48.25.9/143]

STEWART, LEONARD, Bermuda, graduated MD from
Edinburgh University in 1819. [EMG#60]

STEWART, ROBERT, Lieutenant of the 61st Regiment, son of
James Stewart of Urrard, Perthshire, died in Martinique
on 28 June 1795. [CM#11597]

STEWART, WILLIAM, a merchant in Ayr then in Jamaica,
1779. [NAS.CS16.1.175]

STEWART, WILLIAM, Jamaica, married Maria Odelia van
Hoogmert, daughter of Gerevid van Hoogmert a
merchant in La Rochelle, in Edinburgh on 3 January
1780. [Edinburgh Marriage Register]

STEWART, WILLIAM, in Jamaica, 1796, son of James
Stewart, a farmer in Hazlehead. [NAS.RS54.PR38/27]

STEWART, WILLIAM, late in Grenada, now in Inverugie, 4
July 1818. [NAS.RGS#157.23.52]

STILLIE, JOHN, born 1832, only son of George Stillie, died at
Aux Cayes, St Domingo, on 7 July 1853. [EEC#22468]

STIRLING, GEORGE, born 20 August 1768, seventh son of
William Stirling, a merchant in Glasgow, and his wife
Mary Buchanan, died in Jamaica on 15 August 1790.
[Stirlings of Cadder, p.56 {St Andrews, 1933}]

STIRLING, HENRY, born 8 December 1719, third son of Dr
William Stirling and his wife Janet Smith in Glasgow,
died in Jamaica on 9 June 1745. [Stirlings of Cadder,
p.52, {St Andrews, 1933}]

STIRLING, ISABELLA, daughter of Robert Stirling in
Jamaica, married William Trotter, a merchant in
Edinburgh, on 17 June 1781. [Edinburgh Marriage
Register]

STIRLING, JAMES, a merchant in Kingston, Jamaica, 1765. [NAS.GD201.5.130]

STIRLING, JOHN, born 23 February 1768, second son of William Stirling of Cadder, Lanarkshire, educated at Glasgow University in 1789, emigrated to Kingston, Jamaica, in 1789, died in Hampden, Jamaica, on 24 March 1793. [MAGU#128]

STIRLING, PATRICK, at Montego Bay, Jamaica, 1775. [NAS.NRAS#8/24/9]

STIRLING, ROBERT, son of James Stirling of Keir, a merchant in Kingston, Jamaica, in 1746. [Stirlings of Keir, p.539, {Edinburgh, 1858}]; a merchant in Jamaica, was admitted as a burgess and guilds-brother of Ayr on 4 April 1751. [ABR]

STIRLING, ROBERT, merchant in Jamaica, co-owner of the Jane of Glasgow, 1806. [NAS.CE60.11.8/1]

STIRLING, Sir SAMUEL, a planter at King's Bay, Tobago, 1836. [NA.T71/1572]

STIRLING, WILLIAM, of Auchyle, a surgeon in Jamaica, 1732. [NAS.GD171.4209]

STOBO, JOHN, Tortula, graduated MD at Marischal College, Aberdeen, on 3 May 1816. [AUL]

STODDART, GEORGE DOUGLAS, a planter on Calderhall Estate, Tobago, 1836. [NA.T71/1572]

STRACHAN, DAVID, a barber in Port Royal, Jamaica, administration 4 August 1722 New York

STRACHAN, WILLIAM R., son of J. M. Strachan MD in Dollar, Clackmannanshire, died in St Elisabeth's, Jamaica, on 16 August 1860. [S#1638]

STRAITON, THOMAS, a merchant in Jamaica, was admitted as a burgess and guildsbrother of Ayr on 4 April 1751. [ABR]

STRAITON, WILLIAM, a merchant in Jamaica, dead by 1743. [NAS.GD170.3353]

STRANG, JANET, daughter of Walter Strang in Edinburgh, married Reverend George Mitchell, in St George, Grenada, 1862. [S#2126]

STRATON, THOMAS, planter of 8 acres, St Andrew's parish, Jamaica, 1754. [NA.CO137/28]

STUART, JOHN, late in Jamaica, died at 9 Roseberry Terrace, Glasgow, on 2 March 1877. [EC#28838]

STUART, ..., in Jamaica, 1709. [BM.Sloane#4042/65]

SURGEON, JOHN, a gentleman in Jamaica, was admitted as a burgess and guildsbrother of Ayr on 4 April 1751. [ABR]

SUTHERLAND, ARTHUR, in Jamaica, father of James Cubbiston Sutherland who was apprenticed as a writer firstly to A. L. Ramsay, and secondly to John Blair, admitted to the Society of Writers to the Signet on 3 July 1820. ['History of the Society of Writers to H M Signet', Edinburgh, 1890]

SUTHERLAND, ROBERT, of Dunrobin, Jamaica, 1775. [NAS.CS16.1.185'187]

SUTHERLAND, ROBERT, born in Dunrobin in 1776 son of Robert Sutherland and his wife Elizabeth Baillie, settled in St Vincent in 1796, late of St Vincent, 1817, 1824, of Millmount, Ross-shire, died in Hastings, England, 31 October 1828. [NAS.RS54.PR216/228; RS54.1910] [Inverness Journal, 7.11.1828]

SUTHERLAND, ROBERT, born 1805 in Ross-shire, son of George Sackville Sutherland [1770-1812] and Jean MacKay [1772-1858], settled in St Vincent in 1821, a stipendiary magistrate, married Georgina Cumming, father of Robert [1840-1887], died in Kensington, London, 7 March 1883. [Kensington death register, 1883/224]

SUTHERLAND, ..., a merchant, emigrated via Greenock to Jamaica, 1757. [AUL.MS1160.5.12]

SWANSTON, CAROLINE, in St Kitts, 10 April 1833. [NAS.RS.Edinburgh.42/34]

SWANSTON, HELEN, second daughter of James Swanston, Marshall Meadows, Berwickshire, died in St Kitts on 16 February 1869. [S#7999]

SWANSTON, Dr WILLIAM, born 1765, a surgeon and physician in St Kitts, 1800, son of John Swanston, tenant in Seggiedean, [NAS.CS26.910.30]; 5 June 1818. [NAS.RS.Edinburgh.13/99]; died in Edinburgh 7 July 1854. [Greyfriars gravestone, Edinburgh]

SYDSERF, WALTER, in Antigua, 1750s. [NAS.RS.Edin#141/188; 144/1-5; 150/188]

SYLVESTER, GEORGE F., died on Content Estate, Hanover, Jamaica, 24 January 1862. [S#2095]

SYMON, JAMES, born in 1791, a mason, died in Tobago on 5 July 1822. [Inverness Chapel Yard gravestone]

SYMPSON, ALEXANDER, land grant in St Andrew's parish, Dominica, in February 1768. [NAS.GD126/4]

TAILOUR, JOHN, St Kitts, graduated MD at Edinburgh University in 1776. [EUL][EMG#13]

TAIT, WILLIAM, third son of Charles Tait and his wife Mary Erskine in Craigmill, Chapel of Garioch, Aberdeenshire, settled in Jamaica, died at Annetto Bay, St George's, Jamaica, on 5 june 1826. [SAA

TALON, GEORGE, born 1849, son of Rev. T. K. Talon, 2 Bellevue Terrace, Edinburgh, died in Trinidad 29 July 1869. [S#8136]

TANNOCH, THOMAS, an engineer from Glasgow, died in St Lucia, Cuba, during April 1839. [SG#8/781]

TAYLOR, Dr ALEXANDER, a merchant in Grenada, 1776. [NLS#Acc8793]

TAYLOR, ARCHIBALD, from Fife, was admitted as a burgher of St Eustatia, DWI, on 7 August 1780. [NA.CO318/8/83]

TAYLOR, GEORGE, son of James Taylor of Moorfield [1790-1861], died in St Vincent aged 23. [Kilmarnock gravestone]

TAYLOR, JAMES, in Jamaica, formerly a writer in Cupar, Fife, eldest son of William Taylor feuar in Pitlessie, 1800. [NAS.CS26.916.54]

TAYLOR, JAMES R., son of James Taylor in Milton Cottage, Bishopbriggs, late manager of the Barcaldine Estate in Argyll, died in Antigua on 14 June 1853. [EEC#22463][S.27.7.1853]

TAYLOR, JOHN, a merchant in Nevis, 1777. [NLS#MS8793/4]

TAYLOR, JOHN, merchant in Kingston, Jamaica, co-owner of the Mercury of Glasgow 1795. [NAS.CE60.11.4/21]

TAYLOR, SIMON, in Kingston, Jamaica, 1776, [NLS.Acc.8793]; 1780s. [NAS.GD22.SEC.1.314/316]

TELFER, JAMES, in Jamaica, 1779. [NAS.CS16.1.175]

TENANT, AGNES, spouse of David Fraser a merchant in Jamaica, 1771. [NAS.RS27.192.342]

THAIN, ISOBEL, in Grenada, testament 1869 Edinburgh. [NAS.SC70.1.145/561]

THOM, JOHN, a land surveyor, brother of Robert Thom the British Consul in Ningpo, China, died at Middleton Cottage, Clarendon, Jamaica, on 15 May 1851. [AJ#5396]

THOMAS, JOHN, second son of George Thomas a surgeon in Jamaica, matriculated at Glasgow University in 1813. [MUGU#271]

THOMAS, ROBERT, ('Robbert Tomese'), born in Elie, Scotland, married Elisabeth Atwell, widow of Samuel Hicks, born on Nevis, in Curacao, DWI, on 7 March 1719. ['Extract uit het Trouwboek der Gereformeerde Gemeente op het eiland Cuacao van de jaren 1714 tot en met 1722']

THOMSON, ALEXANDER, born in Inverness-shire, possibly resident of St Kitts, married Margarith Flawn of St Eustatia, there on 11 March 1749. ['Afscriften huwelijksakten van St Eustatius van 1710-1750']

THOMSON, ALEXANDER, an attorney in Jamaica, was admitted as a burgess and guildsbrother of Ayr on 4 April 1751. [ABR]

THOMSON, ALEXANDER, Jamaica, married Rachel Pattullo, in Edinburgh on 10 February 1789. [Edinburgh Marriage Register]

THOMSON, ARCHIBALD, a merchant in Nevis, 1778. [NLS#MS8793]

THOMSON, ARCHIBALD, in Jamaica, 3 May 1833. [NAS.RS.Dumbarton#318]

THOMSON, DAVID, a merchant in Kingston, Jamaica, 1761. [NAS.GD180.418]

THOMSON, DUGALD, merchant in Jamaica, 1802. [NAS.RS.Dunbarton#1341]

THOMPSON, Hon. EDWARD, died in Spanish Town, Jamaica, on 20 January 1860. [S#1438]

THOMSON, JAMES, late wright and mason in Kirkton of Blantyre, now in Jamaica, 1742. [NAS.GD1.732.17]

THOMSON, JAMES, born 1765, son of John Thomson a merchant in Dumfries, nephew of baillie Robert Thomson, 44 years in Rio Bueno, Jamaica, died there on 29 May 1831. [PA#106]

THOMSON, JOHN, in Jamaica 1782. [NAS.CS17.1.1/61]

THOMSON, JOHN, born 1793, son of John Thomson a shoemaker in Aberdeen and Margaret Mitchell, died in Jamaica during December 1830. [Banchory Devenick gravestone]

THOMSON, JOHN, of Whitefield Hall, Jamaica, natural son of George Thomson in Aberdeen, died in May 1839. [NAS.PS3.16/59]

THOMSON, JOHN, in Jamaica, later in Montrose, testament confirmed on 2 March 1814 with the Commissariot of Brechin. [NAS.CC3/126]

THOMSON, JOHN, of Whitefield Hall, Jamaica, 1839, son of George Thomson in Aberdeen. [NAS.PS3.16.59]

THOMSON, JOHN, born in Aberdeen during 1821, master of the barque Ellon of London, died at Port Morant, Jamaica, on 8 February 1852. [AJ:7.4.1852]

THOMSON, JONATHAN, born 1730 in Kirkhill, Inverness, son of Reverend Robert Thomson and his wife Mary Calder, died in Jamaica on 2 December 1748. [F.5.473]

THOMSON, KENNETH, born on 29 December 1766 in Durness, son of Reverend John Thomson and his wife Mary Robertson, died in Kingston, Jamaica, on 24 July 1794. [F.7.102]

THOMSON, MACKAY, born on 11 December 1784 in Durness, son of Reverend John Thomson and his wife Mary Robertson, died in Kingston, Jamaica, during 1803. [F.7.102]

THOMSON, PETER, eldest son of John Thomson in Burntisland, Fife, died in Kingston, Jamaica, on 11 February 1803. [GM.72.374]

THOMSON, ROBERT, in Nevis, 1776. [NLS.Acc.8793]

THOMSON, ROBERT, late of Jamaica, married Jane Kennedy, daughter of the late Robert Kennedy of Daljarrock, in Maybole, Ayrshire, in January 1796. [CM#11599][NAS.RD2.271.479]

THOMSON, ROBERT CRAIG, of Sion House, Kingston, Jamaica, died in Manchester, Jamaica, on 9 February 1854. [S.15.3.1854][EEC#22554]

THOMSON, THOMAS, in New Providence, co-owner of the Garland of Glasgow, 1801. [NAS.CE60.11.7/77]

THOMSON, WILLIAM, in St Kitts, 1776, [NLS.Acc.8793/42]; deceased, late in St Kitts, husband of Mary Thomson in Edinburgh, 1821. [NAS.CS17.1.40/173]

THOMSON, WILLIAM, from Jamaica, died in Bath during 1817. [S#16]

THORBURN, ADAM WILLIAM, a planter in Clarendon, Jamaica, 1828. [NAS.CS17.1.47/242]

TODD, JAMES, born 23 February 1809, fourth son of John Todd, died in Belmont, Grenada, on 18 August 1853. [Kirkmaiden gravestone, Wigtownshire]

TODD, JAMES REEVES, MD, born 1840, medical officer of the districts of St John and St Marks, died in Charlottetown, Grenada, on 4 August 1867. [S#7511]

TODD, MARGARET ANN, daughter of James Todd, was born in San Fernando, Trinidad, on 23 December 1848 and died there on 31 December 1848. [SG#18/1793]

TOLAND, JOHN, born in 1828, son of Hugh and Lobetia Toland, an engineer, applied to settle in Havana, Cuba, on 12 October 1856. [NAC.Cartas de Domocilio]

TOP, ADAM, late in Jamaica, died at 53 Constitution Street, Aberdeen, on 26 August 1868. [S#7824]

TORRANCE, ANNABELLA DOUGLAS, born in Kilmarnock, Ayrshire, on 2 March 1821, wife of Reverend W. O. Allan, died on St Thomas, Danish Virgin Islands, on 29 June 1862. [St Thomas gravestone]

TOSHACH, WILLIAM, St Thomas in the East, Surrey County, Jamaica, 1776. [DCA:H1620]

TOWER, JAMES, in St Croix, 1776. [NLS.Acc.8793/30]

TOWER, JAMES, son of John Tower in Aberdeen, educated at Marischal College, Aberdeen, from 1774 to 1778, graduated MD, late of St Thomas, West Indies, died in Logie, Crimond, Aberdeenshire, on 8 May 1818. [St Nicholas gravestone, Aberdeen][MCA.II.347]

TOWER, JOHN, formerly in St Croix, died in Aberdeen on 3 April 1799. [St Nicholas gravestone, Aberdeen]

TRAILL, WILLIAM, in Dominica, son of John Traill late tenant farmer in Strathkinness, Fife, and his first wife Isabel Stewart, 28 November 1793. [NAS.SC20.36.16]

TRAN, HUGH, son of Arthur Tran in Glasgow, to St Kitts 1767, a merchant in St Kitts, 1779, 1782, in Dominica 1783. [NAS.CS17.1.1/282; 2/247][GA.B10.15.7141]; [NAS.CS16.1.174]; a merchant in Glasgow and St Kitts, heir to his mother Elizabeth Warden, 3 June 1768. [NAS.B64.1.9.134/9]

TRAVERS, HORACE, Assistant Commissary General, died in Jamaica on 26 June 1867. [S#7487]

TROTTER, JOHN, a merchant in Kingston, Jamaica, 1755. [NAS.AC7/47/598]

TROTTER, JOHN, in Antigua 1760. [DA.Ogilvie pp/30]

TROTTER, JOHN, in Dominica, died 1808, testament 2 November 1825 Edinburgh. [NAS.CC8.11.VII/36]

TROUP, GEORGE, in Jamaica, 1788. [NAS.NRAS#1368/118]

TUCKER, THOMAS, Bermuda, graduated MD from
   Edinburgh University in 1770. [EMG#10]
TUDHOPE, JEAN, widow of William Tudhope a late surgeon
   in Antigua, 1794. [ECA.Moses#172/6745]
TULLIDEPH WALTER, a surgeon in Antigua 1735, 1760
   [BM.Sloane#3984/36; 4049/3][DA.Ogilvie pp48]
TULLOCH, ROBERT, son of Dr James Tulloch a physician in
   Jamaica, was apprenticed to William Brown in
   Edinburgh on 28 November 1799. [Edinburgh
   Apprentice Register]
TURING, Reverend INGLIS, born 1743, son of reverend
   Alexander Turing and Anna Brown in Foveran, Rector of
   St Thomas in the Vale, Jamaica, died in November
   1791. [Glasgow Courier#57][GM.61.1235]
TURNBULL, PETER, a planter in Montserrat, then in
   Greenock, 1791, [NAS.RS81/15]; his will refers to wife
   Margaret Lyle, his daughter Mary, his sister Margery
   Stevenson and her children, his friend Robert Turner in
   Greenock, will subscribed on 22 June 1809, registered
   20 February 1816 in Renfrew. [NAS.SC53.56.1/57]
TURNER, WILLIAM, Jamaica, graduated MD from Edinburgh
   University in 1819. [EMG#63]
TYRE, JOHN, a merchant in Tortula, 1800. [GA:T-ARD#13/1]
URE, JOHN, jr., from Glasgow, died at Aux Cayes, St
   Domingo, 10 June 1820. [GkAd#2427]
URQUHART, JOHN MATTHESON, died in Tobago on 9 April
   1853. [EEC#22440]
VINT, WILLIAM, in Jamaica, son of Thomas Vint, Craigflower,
   1794. [NAS.RS.Fife#4031]
WADDELL, JAMES, a merchant in Jamaica, father of James
   Waddell born 1816 who was educated at Edinburgh
   Academy from 1824 to 1828. [EAR]
WADDELL, Mrs, relict of Matthew Waddell in Jamaica, died in
   Lanark during 1817. [S#18]
WALKER, W. P., a surgeon, son of David Walker a farmer in
   Upper Park, Aberdeenshire, died in Grenada on 27
   October 1838. [AJ: 30.1.1839]
WALKER, ANN, relict of Dr James Walker in Jamaica, died
   19 July 1836. [AJ#4620]
WALKER, GEORGE, in Antigua 1753. [NAS.CS96/644]
WALKER, ISABELLA, born 4 September 1771 in Collessie,
   Fife, daughter of Reverend William Walker and his wife
   Margaret Manderston, married Paul Samuels in

Jamaica, [F.5.135]; relict of Paul Stevens Samuells of
Negril Spots, Jamaica, died at 15 Rutland Street,
Edinburgh, on 9 February 1853. [EEC#22393]

WALKER, JAMES, born 2 october 1791, second son of
William Walker of Dempsterton, Fife, and his wife Allison
Lyon, died in Jamaica during 1813. [Lyons of Cossin
and West Ogil, {Edinburgh, 1901}]

WALKER, MARGARET, third daughter of Hugh Walker in
Jamaica, married Dr James Stewart of Tulloch, in
Edinburgh on 3 August 1840. [AJ#4831]

WALKER, WILLIAM, late in Antigua, then in St Vincent, 1778.
[NAS.CS16.1.173]

WALLACE, HUGH, son of the late Thomas Wallace of
Cairnhill, now in Westmoreland parish, Jamaica, 1764.
[NAS.RS81/7/167]

WALLACE, HUGH, in Biscany, Jamaica, 1820.
[NAS.CS239/W36/1; CS96.4515]

WALLACE, HUGH RITCHIE, born in Glasgow, eldest son of
Hugh Wallace of Biscany, a gentleman in Jamaica,
matriculated at Glasgow University in 1802.
[MAGU#201]

WALLACE, JAMES, in Jamaica, was admitted as a burgess
of Edinburgh in 1749. [Edinburgh Burgess Roll]

WALLACE, JAMES, born in 1789, son of John Wallace a
teacher, died in Jamaica on 23 January 1820.
[Blackfriars gravestone, Glasgow]

WALLACE, JAMES, Kingston, Jamaica, married Anne Maria
brooks niece of John Smith, Salisbury Plain, St
Andrews, Jamaica, at Halfway Tree Church, St
Andrews, Jamaica, on 12 January 1830. [PA#35]

WALLACE, JOHN, 1712-1805, a West Indian merchant,
second son of Thomas Wallace of Cairnhill, Kilmarnock,
Ayrshire, married (1) Anne Murdoch, (2) Jean
Porterfield, a planter in Jamaica who returned to
Glasgow in 1770. [GA]

WALLACE, WILLIAM, a merchant in Jamaica, was admitted
as a burgess of Edinburgh in 1752. [Edinburgh Burgess
Roll]

WALLACE, WILLIAM, a planter in Tobago, 1778.
[NLS#MS8794]

WALLACE, Dr ...., to Montserrat in 1730.
[NAS.GD237/12/35/6]

WALLEN, JOHN, son of Matthew Wallen in Jamaica, graduated MA at Marischal College, Aberdeen, in 1773. [MCA.II.346]

WARDEN, JAMES, a merchant in St Kitts, 1778. [NAS.CS16.1.173/322]

WARDEN, ROBERT, in St Jago, Cuba, and his wife Mary Alexander in Greenock, 1823. [NAS.SC53.56.3]

WARDROP, JOHN, from Glasgow, was admitted as a burgher of St Eustatia, DWI, on 8 August 1781. [NA.CO318/8/83]

WARRAND, JAMES, died on Dougaldston Estate, Grenada, on 15 September 1838. [AJ#4742]

WARREN, JOHN, a planter in Jamaica, 1776. [NLS#MS8794/5]

WATHERSTON, JOHN, formerly in Greenlaw, late of Jamaica, dead by 1808. [NAS.GD2.384]

WATHERSTONE, ARCHIBALD, in Trinidad, 1821. [NAS.CS17.1.40/180]

WATSON, ANDREW, son of John Watson in Jamaica, educated at Marischal College, Aberdeen, from 1779 to 1783. later a schoolmaster and minister in Tarland, Aberdeenshire. [MCA.II.355]

WATSON, ISABELLA, widow of John Cullen late of the Bengal Horse Artillery, died in Jamaica on 22 June 1834. [AJ#4511]

WATSON, JAMES, from Johnstone, Renfrewshire, a divinity student in 1823, later a minister in Kingston, Jamaica. [AUPC]

WATSON, JOHN, son of Captain Andrew Watson, a merchant in Kingston, Jamaica, was admitted as a burgess of Edinburgh in 1792. [Edinburgh Burgess Roll]

WATSON, JOHN, Jamaica, married Ann Baillie Wood, born 19 June 1782 in Rosemarkie, daughter of Reverend Alexander Wood and his wife Janet Houstoun, in Jamaica during 1805. [F.7.23]

WATSON, WILLIAM, late in Jamaica, died in Perth during April 1786. [GM#IX.420.21]

WATT, Mrs AGNES GLENNIE, from Inverurie, Aberdeenshire, died in St George's Plain Estate, Savanna-la-Mar, Jamaica, on 8 September 1865. [AJ:4.11.1863]

WATT, ANTOINETTE LOUISE JOSEPHINE, eldest daughter of Henry David Watt, died in Roseau, Dominica, on 2 June 1860. [S#1597]

WATT, EDWARD LINDSAY, Jamaica, graduated MD from Edinburgh University in 1818. [EMG#57]

WATT, JAMES, from Cairnie, Aberdeenshire, died on Montreuil Estate, Grenada, on 29 August 1863. [AJ:4.11.1863]

WATT, JOHN, Jamaica, graduated MD from Edinburgh University in 1809. [EMG#42]

WATT, PETER, husband of Agnes Glennie Watt, died in Jamaica on 12 September 1865. [AJ:4.11.1863]

WATT, ROBERT, Jamaica, graduated MD from Edinburgh University in 1803. [EMG#34]

WATT, ROBERT, Member of Assembly for St Elizabeth, died at Montego Bay, Jamaica, on 8 March 1841. [GSP#654]

WATT, ..., daughter of Henry D. Watt, was born on Chiltern Estate, Dominica, on 10 July 1855. [EEC#322778]

WAUCHOPE, MARY RIDDELL, late of Jamaica, died in Maybank, Loanhead, on 22 October 1839. [AJ#4780]

WAUGH, PATRICK, in Jamaica, 1811. [NAS.GD171.985]

WAUGH, PETER, son of Thomas Waugh a merchant in Leith, died in Jamaica during May 1807. [DPCA#262]

WEBSTER, JOHN, jr., from Greenock to Antigua on the Joanna, master James Brown, 9 September 1790. [NAS.E504.15.56]

WEBSTER, THOMAS, a servant, died in Jamaica during June 1749. [AJ#107]

WEDDERBURN, JOHN, in Hanover, Jamaica, son of John Wedderburn of Blackness, granted the lands of Idvies on 6 August 1766. [NAS.RGS.109.12; RS35.xv.104]; 1772, [DCA: H1931]

WEDDERBURN, JOHN, born 18 August 1776 in Inveresk, son of James Wedderburn, educated at Glasgow University in 1789, emigrated to Jamaica in 1794, died there on 19 May 1799. [MAGU#157]

WEDDERSPOON, LAURENCE, born 1701, died 25 April 1788. [Tennant's Estate gravestone, Claredon, Jamaica]

WEIR, JOHN, land grant in St Andrew's parish, Dominica, in February 1768. [NAS.GD126/4]

WEIR, ROBERT, Unity Estate, Portland parish, Jamaica, 1790. [NAS.CS16.1.173/416]

WELCH, ..., son of Rev. John Welch, was born in Goshen,

Jamaica, on 10 November 1869. [S#8232]

WELSH, JAMES, in Kingston, Jamaica, was admitted as a burgess of Arbroath, Angus, in 1789. [Arbroath Burgess Roll]

WELSH, ..., daughter of James Welsh, was born on Dupuys Estate, St Kitts, on 29 October 1863. [S#2639]

WELSH, ..., daughter of James Welsh, was born in Needsmust Estate, St Kitts, 22 November 1868. [S#7918]

WEMYSS, DAVID, in St Kitts, 1776. [NLS.Acc.8793]

WEST, JOHN, born 10 April 1756 in Logie, Fife, son of Reverend West and his wife Margaret Mein, educated at St Andrews University in 1776, a minister who emigrated to Jamaica in 1785, died there on 17 October 1817. [EMA#62][FPA.21.316]

WEST, MAURICE, merchant in Kingston, Jamaica, co-owner of the Commerce of Glasgow, 1793; the Alexander of Glasgow, 1694; the Brothers of Glasgow 1798; the Britannia of Glasgow, 1799; the Ariadne of Glasgow, 1799, the Swinger of Glasgow, 1800; the Mary of Glasgow, 1803. [NAS.CE60.11.3/65,72; 5/21; 6/1/67/106; 8/27]

WHITE, JOHN, St Elizabeth's, Jamaica, 1811. [NAS.GD2.252]

WHITECROSS, JESSIE HELEN, daughter of William Whitecross, a United Presbyterian minister, and his wife Margaret Brown who were married in Ayr on 23 February 1857, was born at sea in the Caribbean aboard the Thomas James on 14 November 1857. [NRH.MRB]

WHITEFORD, JOHN, of Fala, Blackshiels, born 1819, died at Porto Plata, Santo Domingo, 19 November 1861. [S#2071]

WHITEHEAD, WILLIAM, in Antigua, 1761. [DA.Ogilvie.ms.p56]

WHITELAW, JOHN, jr., son of John Whitelaw a perfumer in Glasgow, in St Vincent 1800. [NAS.CS18.706.26]

WHITELAW, THOMAS, late in Jamaica now in Glasgow, 1782. [NAS.CS17.1.1/61]

WHITELAW and WILSON, merchants in St Vincent, 1799. [NAS.GD237.12.25]

WHYTE, FRANCES, youngest daughter of Charles Whyte of the 60th Regiment, died in St Vincent on 17 May 1834. [AJ#4518]

WHYTE, JAMES SHAND, eldest son of Reverend Alexander Whyte in Fettercairn, Kincardineshire, died in Gouyave, Grenada, on 14 December 1859. [DC#23470][S#1436]

WIGHT, CHARLES, a merchant in Jamaica, 18 April 1833. [NAS.RS.Edinburgh.42/47]

WIGHT, ROBERT, in Jamaica, 1821. [NAS.CS17.1.40/292]

WIGHTMAN, CHARLES, a merchant in Tobago, son of Charles Wightman a merchant in Anstruther, Fife, 1778. [NAS.CS16.1.174]

WIGHTMAN, CHARLES, a planter in Tobago, 1805, [GA:T-ARD#13/1]

WILKIE, PATRICK, in St Vincent, 1776. [NLS.Acc.8793]

WILKIE, THOMAS, a merchant in Glasgow then in Kingston, Jamaica, testament confirmed with the Commissariat of Edinburgh on 22 November 1794. [NAS.CC8.8.129]

WILKINSON, JOHN, a merchant in New Providence, 1821. [NAS.CS17.1.40/261]

WILLIAMSON, ALEXANDER, in Jamaica, then in the Haughs of Edinglassie, testament confirmed with the Commissariat of Aberdeen on 23 December 1791. [NAS]

WILLIAMSON, JOHN, born 23 April 1780, son of Reverend John Williamson and his wife Janet ...., a surgeon in St James, Jamaica. [F.2.298]

WILLIAMSON, ROBERT, husband of Catherine Campbell, to Jamaica, captain of the 3rd West Indian Regiment, died in Jamaica 1798. [NAS.CS26.911.10]

WILLIAMSON, SINCLAIR, a merchant at Ocho Rios Bay, St Ann's, Jamaica, died in Cuba during June 1809. [PC#34]

WILLIAMSON, THOMAS, in St Elizabeth's, Jamaica, 1822. [NAS.SC49.48.25.18/100]

WILLIAMSON, WILLIAM, educated at King's College, Aberdeen, later a clergyman in Jamaica by 1792. [FPA#316]

WILLIAMSON, WILLIAM, in New Providence, co-owner of the Garland of Glasgow, 1801. [NAS.CE60.11.7/77]

WILLOX, ALEXANDER, in Antigua, 1761. [DA.Ogilvie.ms.p54]

WILSON, ADAM, son of John Wilson in Montgrew, Banffshire, died in Bossue, Manchester, Jamaica, on 10 November 1850. [AJ#5374]

WILSON, ALEXANDER, of Shieldhall, in Grenada, 1776. [NLS.Acc8793/2]

WILSON, BARCLAY, Provost Marshal of Tobago, died there on 1 October 1831. [PA#117]

WILSON, GEORGE, merchant in Grenada, co-owner of the Laurel of Glasgow, 1795; the Minerva of Glasgow and the Diana of Glasgow, 1798; the Leander of Greenock, 1799; the Garland of Glasgow 1801 [NAS.CE6011.4/42; 5/3; 6/59; 7/77]

WILSON, HENRY BROUNCKER, St Kitts, graduated MD from Edinburgh University in 1784. [EMG#17]

WILSON, JAMES, in St Vincent 1796. [NAS.GD237.12.25]; in 1800 [NAS.CS18.706.26]

WILSON, JEANNIE, born in 1846, daughter of the late Alexander Milne in the Mains of Esslemont, Aberdeenshire, died in St Joseph's, Trinidad, on 16 December 1874. [AJ:20.1.1875]

WILSON, JOHN, St Maartens, graduated MD from Edinburgh University in 1795. [EMG#26]

WILSON, JOHN, son of John Wilson in Montgrew, Banffshire, died in Bossue, Manchester, Jamaica, on 5 December 1850. [AJ#5374]

WILSON, JOHN, died in Georgia, Jamaica, on 12 July 1878. [EC#29317]

WILSON, JOHN FLEMING, eldest son of George Wilson late of Martin and Wilson, died in St Croix 2 February 1868. [S#7791]

WILSON, PATRICK, in St Martins, Dutch West Indies, 1753. [NAS.CS96/644]

WILSON, PHILIP, a planter in St Kitts, 1780, son of William Wilson of Soonhope a writer in Edinburgh, 1780. [NAS.CS16.1.179]

WILSON, RICHARD, in St Kitts, 1757. [NAS.GD237/12/47]

WILSON, ROBERT, planter of 12 acres, St Andrew's parish, Jamaica, 1754. [NA.CO137/28]

WILSON, ROBERT, born 26 February 1791 in Cluny, son of Nathaniel Wilson, farmer at the Mill of Kincardine, and his wife Euphemia Angus, died in Jamaica on 19 December 1814. [Aboyne gravestone]

WILSON, ROBERT, a shipmaster and merchant in Tortula, dead by 1800. [GA.T-ARD#13/1]

WILSON, THOMAS, in Tobago, 1776. [NLS.Acc8793/26]

WILSON, ..., daughter of F. W. G. Wilson, born in Lucca, Jamaica, on 4 April 1851. [AJ#5392]

WINCHESTER, WILLIAM, planter of 500 acres, St Andrew's parish, Jamaica, 1754. [NA.CO137/28]

WISHART, DANIEL, from Aberdeen, chief mate of the barque John King of Glasgow, died in Jamaica on 26 September 1857. [AJ:6.1.1858]

WOOD, JOHN, Jamaica, married Isobel Philip, in Edinburgh on 21 June 1761. [Edinburgh Marriage Register]

WOOD, JOHN, a merchant in St Kitts, 1790. [NAS.CS16.1.173/428]

WOOD, JOHN, born 28 June 1797, son of Reverend Charles Wood and his wife Mary Gray, died in Jamaica on 13 January 1819. [F.3.322]

WOOD, SOPHIA, born 4 October 1775 in Rosemarkie, daughter of Reverend Alexander Wood and his wife Janet Houstoun, married James Fowler of Grange, in Jamaica 1792. [F.7.23]

WOOD, WILLIAM, sometime in Jamaica, then in Port Glasgow, 1807. [NAS.RD.Renfrew#8647][NAS.SC58.1.9]

WORDIE, JAMES, born in 1799, third son of Thomas Wordie a craftsman in Denny, matriculated at Glasgow University in 1709, minister at the Scots Church in Kingston, Jamaica, from 1823 to 1842, and in Cupar, Fife, from 1844 to 1862, died on 3 August 1862. [MAGU#241]

WRIGHT, ISABEL, spouse of James Henderson, in St Vincent, 1782. [NAS.CS17.1.1/78]

WRIGHT, JAMES, born 1818, son of Simon Wright and Margaret Dunnet, died in the West Indies on 22 July 1856. [St Devenick on the Hill gravestone]

WRIGHT, JOHN, a merchant in Jamaica, was admitted as a burgess and guildsbrother of Ayr on 4 April 1751. [ABR]

WRIGHT, ROBERT B., Jamaica, graduated MD from Edinburgh University in 1803. [EMG#40]

WYKE, ANTONY, son of Antony Wyke in Antigua, educated at Marischal College, Aberdeen, 1782. [MCA.II.358]

WYLLIE, WILLIAM, a planter on Greenhill Estate,Tobago, 1836. [NA.T71/1572]

YOUNG, DAVID, in Grenada, 1776. [NLS.Acc8793/1]
YOUNG, Miss EDMONSTONE, from Glasgow, died in
    Kingston, Jamaica, in 1817. [S#19]
YOUNG, FRANCIS, born 4 Mar.1848, son of Matthew Young
    schoolmaster [1818-1873] and Sarah Tebbett [1825-
    1874], died in Richmond, Tobago, 9 January 1871.
    [Straiton gravestone]
YOUNG, JAMES, planter of 300 acres, St Andrew's parish,
    Jamaica, 1754. [NA.CO137/28]
YOUNG, JAMES, Pimento Grove, St Dorothy, Jamaica, son
    of John Young in Glasgow, died in Jamaica on 12
    October 1838. [SG#8/745]
YOUNG, ROBERT, in Nassau, New Providence, 5 March
    1811. [NAS.RS.Edinburgh.3/23]
YOUNG, ROBERT BOYD, Tobago, graduated MD in
    Aberdeen on 18 May 1811. [AUL]
YOUNG, THOMAS, of Youngfield, formerly a surgeon in
    Tortula, then in London, 1763.
    [NAS.RS.Dumfries.XIX.451]
YOUNG, WILLIAM, born Uphall, West Lothian, settled and
    died in Trelawney parish, Cornwall County, Jamaica, will
    dated 28 March 1815. [NAS.RH1.2.804]
YOUNGER, THOMAS, born 16 August 1747, son of Andrew
    Younger and his wife Helen House, from Glasgow, late
    of Wilmington, North Carolina, died in Lucie, Jamaica, in
    1795. [GC:12.9.1795][GM.65.794]
YUILLE, ANDREW, in Jamaica, 1783. [NAS.CS17.1.2/245]
YUILLE, ROBERT, in Antigua, 1754. [NAS.CS96/647]

SEVENTEENTH CENTURY ADDENDUM

ABERCROMBIE, Reverend THOMAS, with wife Anne and a
child, from London to Bermuda on the ketch
Prosperous, arrived 2 September 1661, settled in
Glebeland, Tuckers Town, died before 1663. [BS]

BEATON, JOHN, [?][Jan Bieton], on St Thomas Island,
Danish West Indies, 1686. [St Thomas tax roll]

BLAIR, JOHN, ('Johan Blaer'), a planter on St Thomas, 1686,
[St Thomas Tax Roll, 1686]; with his Dutch wife Anna
David, and two children Gillis Blair and Robert Blair, in
1688. [1688 Census of the Danish West Indies]

CAMPBELL, COLIN, in Jamaica, 1699.
[NAS.NRAS#2177/1416]

CAMPBELL, JOHN, a petitioner in Antigua 20 September
1664. [SPAWI.1664/234]

CHALMERS, JAMES, a merchant in St Kitts, was admitted as
a burgess and guildsbrother of Ayr on 20 December
1665. [ABR]

COCHRANE, JOHN, in Montserrat, 1696. [NA.Association
Oath Rolls]

COHOUNE, JOHN, with 11 acres in St Andrew's parish,
Jamaica, 1670. [SPAWI.1670/270]

COLLINSON, ROBERT, son of William Collinson, a
gentleman in St Kitts was admitted as a burgess and
guilds-brother of Ayr on 20 December 1685. [ABR]

CORBETT, WILLIAM, at Halfway Tree, St Kitts, 1667.
[NA.CO1.42/193]

CROOKSHANK, FRANCIS, with 40 acres in St Katherine's
parish, Jamaica, 1670. [SPA.1670/70]

CROOKSHANK, JAMES, with 90 acres in St Katherine's
parish, Jamaica, 1670. [SPA.1670/270]

CRUICKSHANK, JAMES, a chaplain bound for the Leeward
Islands on 28 February 1694. [CTB#X.1.514]

DUNKIN, GEORGE, with 60 acres in St Katherine's parish,
Jamaica, 1670. [SPA.1670.270]

EDWARD, DAVID, (?), ["Davit Edwort"], witness in Curacao,
20 August 1641. [NY.Hist.MS.Dutch.Vol.II, 1642-1647,
Reg. of Provl.Sec.]

FERGUSON, ROBERT, with 4 acres in St Thomas parish,
Jamaica, in 1670. [SPAWI.1670/270]

FRAME, WILLIAM, with 10 acres in Clarendon parish,
Jamaica, 1670. [SPA.1670/270]

FRIZELL, JOHN, with 600 acres in St John's parish, Jamaica, in 1670. [SPA.1670/270]

FULLERTON, GEORGE, in Montserrat, 1696.
[NA.Association Oath Rolls]

GALLOWAY, ROBERT, with 9.75 acres in St Andrew's parish, Jamaica, 1670. [SPAWI.1670.270]

GUNN, JOHN, at Halfway Tree, St Kitts, 1667.
[NA.CO1.42/193]

GUNN, JOSEPH, with 90 acres in St John's parish, Jamaica, 1670. [SPA.1670/270]

HAMILTON, ALEXANDER, in Montserrat, 1696.
[NA.Association Oath Rolls]

HAMILTON, JOHN, in Antigua, 1696. [NA.Association Oath Rolls]

HAMILTON, W., in Nevis 1696. [NA.Association Oath Rolls]

HENDERSON, Captain ARCHIBALD, settled as a planter in Antigua during the 1660s. [SPAWI.1672/806]

HOME, JOHN, with 6 acres in St Andrew's parish, Jamaica, in 1670. [SPAWI.1670/270]

INNES, ALEXANDER, a chaplain sent to the Leeward Islands on 28 February 1694. [CTB.X.1/514]

JOHNSTON, JAMES, brother of Thomas Johnston a merchant in Glasgow, died in Montserrat during 1684. [NAS.RD2.104.958]

LAWDER, GEORGE, in St Thomas, Middle Island, St Kitts, 1667. [NA.CO1.42/193]

LINDSAY, ALEXANDER, a factor in Barbados and St Kitts for Archibald Hay, 1649. [NAS.GD34.948]

MCALESTER, CHARLES, subscribed 3 April 1666, died aged 85, probate 7 May 1672 Barbados. [RB6/8/393]

MACALL, ANDREW, subscribed 23 February 1654, probate 20 October 1658 Barbados. [RB6/13/264]

MCARTHUR, JOHN, in St Kitts, 1696. [NA.Association Oath Rolls]

MACFARLANE, MALCOLM, (?), ["Mackum Mackparly"], a witness in Curacao, 20 August 1641.
[NY.Hist.MS.Dutch, Vol.II, 1642-1647]

MCGILL, JOHN, with 90 acres in Clarendon parish, Jamaica, 1670. [SPAWI.1670/270]

MACKINNEN, DANIEL, in Antigua, 1696. [NA.Association Oath Rolls]

MARSHALL, ALEXANDER, (?), ["Alexander Merchall"], witness in Curacao 20 August 1641. [NY Hist.MS, Dutch, Vol.II,1642-1647, Reg.of Provl. Sec.]

NESMITH, Captain Robert, at Halfway Tree, St Kitts, 1667. [NA.CO1.42/193]

REID, EDWARD, with 30 acres in St David's parish, Jamaica, 1670. [SPAWI.1670/70]

REID, THOMAS, with 150 acres in St David's parish, Jamaica, 1670. [SPAWI.1670/270]

ROLLAND, ROBERT, a merchant burgess of Ayr, died in St Kitts in 1646. [testament 23.11.1648/4.8.1649 Commissariat of Glasgow]

SCOTT, JAMES, with 17 acres in St Thomas parish, Jamaica, 1670. [SPAWI.1670/70]

STEELE, THOMAS, in Jamaica, 1699. [NAS.GD3.5.812]

STEELE, WILLIAM, in St Thomas, Middle Island, St Kitts, 1667. [NA.CO1.42/193]

WATSON, ALEXANDER, at Halfway Tree, St Kitts, 1667. [NA.CO1.42/193]

WATSON, ALEXANDER, a merchant burgess of Glasgow, to Jamaica in 1668, died on Nevis. [NAS.Unextracted processes, 1671]

WOODROPP, WILLIAM, at Halfway Tree, St Kitts, 1667. [NA.CO1.42/19

www.ingramcontent.com/pod-product-compliance
Lightning Source LLC
Chambersburg PA
CBHW061750270326
41928CB00011B/2455

* 9 780806 353128 *